Micro Media Industries

Micro Media Industries

Hmong American Media Innovation in the Diaspora

LORI KIDO LOPEZ

Rutgers University Press

New Brunswick, Camden, and Newark, New Jersey, and London

Library of Congress Cataloging-in-Publication Data

Names: Lopez, Lori Kido, author.
Title: Micro media industries : Hmong American media innovation in the
    diaspora / Lori Kido Lopez.
Description: New Brunswick : Rutgers University Press, 2021. |
    Includes bibliographical references and index.
Identifiers: LCCN 2020051456 | ISBN 9781978823341 (paperback) |
    ISBN 9781978823358 (hardcover) | ISBN 9781978823365 (epub) |
    ISBN 9781978823372 (mobi) | ISBN 9781978823389 (pdf)
Subjects: LCSH: Hmong American mass media. | Hmong Americans in mass media.
Classification: LCC P94.5.H5942 U656 2021 | DDC 302.23089/95972073—dc23
LC record available at https://lccn.loc.gov/2020051456

A British Cataloging-in-Publication record for this book is available from the British Library.

♾ The paper used in this publication meets the requirements of the American National
Standard for Information Sciences—Permanence of Paper for Printed Library Materials,
ANSI Z39.48-1992.

www.rutgersuniversitypress.org

Manufactured in the United States of America

For Mom and Dad

Contents

Contents

Micro Media Industries

1

Introduction
· ·
The Significance of Micro
Media Industries

Hmong Americans seeking media created by and for their people are faced with
a rich and multifaceted array of offerings. There are radio programs with current affairs and news programming, musical performances of traditional music
and contemporary pop songs, and numerous social media networks for Hmong
storytelling. There are websites for meeting other Hmong people, for buying
and selling items, and for learning about Hmong language and Hmong customs. In the Twin Cities, stacks of Hmong newspapers and magazines line the
racks outside of bustling markets and businesses. Stalls at Hmong markets and
festivals sell hundreds of DVDs, with movies ranging in genre from drama and
romance to horror and comedy. Yet the wide variety of media available belies
the struggles that Hmong people have faced in building sustainable media
industries, as the financial models that support media production often rely on
resources that are in short supply for this relatively small ethnic community.

Moreover, Hmong in the diaspora have needed to build their media industries from the ground up, rather than being able to connect to an already established national media infrastructure. For diasporic populations originating
from countries such as India, Mexico, Russia, China, or the Philippines, media
use often means finding a way to connect back to the popular media created
within their homeland via satellite, mobile platforms, or other digital technologies. Diasporic media provide a way to connect with members of a community

who may be geographically dispersed so that they can maintain a sense of their own specific identity, heritage, and culture while also providing news and information in their native languages. Yet this is not possible for those among the 1975 Hmong diaspora, who largely trace their origins to Laos or Thailand—countries in which Hmong remain ethnic minorities, at 8 percent of the Lao population and around 1 percent of the Thai population. Due to the lack of a home country, Hmong media power remains limited as a whole, subsisting with scarce community resources or support. If this is the case, how have Hmong American media industries been able to thrive and proliferate?

Through its investigation of the nuances and contours of Hmong American media practices, this book shows how a small population with limited resources can find ways to deploy new media technologies in order to maintain a media ecology that resembles the mainstream. I focus specifically on the way that Hmong media industries consist almost exclusively of what I term "micro media industries." These small-scale media run by extremely limited staff evolve in ways that are culturally specific and can nimbly adapt to the changing needs of a community in flux. Moreover, they serve to critique the high barriers for entry that are necessary for maintaining traditional forms of media industry in a labor market that values population size above nearly all other metrics. While we might assume that certain micro media industries mark a temporary moment before resource limitations can be overcome, an alternative perspective is that their innovations can be seen as a model that other media industries can integrate into their own practices. Media evolution can take winding and counterintuitive paths, and does not necessarily move in a linear fashion toward commodification, capitalization, and growth. Indeed, there are many other examples of micro media industries that are already thriving today and this deep dive into Hmong media can help us to better understand them. In peeling back the curtain on a set of outlets that are small and necessarily constricted, we can see the possibilities that are opened up within these flexible and mobile industries while also considering the limitations that accompany them.

This book argues that micro media industries, rather than being dismissed for their small size and ostensible lack of resources, ought to be held up as models of media innovation that can expose both the possibilities and limitations engendered by super niche media production. This includes running media outlets with extremely small staffs, sometimes of just a single micro media entrepreneur, and mastering multiple skills related to production and distribution. The micro media entrepreneurs investigated here also pursue innovative business models with goals that can be outside of commodification, capitalization, and growth. Some participate in traditional media platforms like television and radio, while others develop new forms altogether—including hybrid media platforms that harness the affordances of existing technologies and evolve rapidly to meet an audience population's special needs. Rather than seeing the techniques used by micro media industries as anomalous measures that have to be taken under constricted circumstances, they could serve as models for other media industries and audience populations which may similarly trend more "micro" in the future.

The Hmong American media landscape as documented in this book demonstrates the wide array of possibilities afforded by micro media industries. Participating in the creation of media that is by and for themselves offers new routes to self-representation, which sometimes highlights the experiences of marginalized community members such as Hmong women and queer Hmong folks. This emphasis on visibility and community empowerment for minority groups can be one of the central goals of micro media outlets, contesting expectations that media outlets must be financially profitable. Micro media industries can also serve as a proof of concept for new platforms and uses of media technology. But this investigation also exposes the limitations Hmong micro media entrepreneurs face in developing media outlets. This includes struggles around the concentration of media power in a small number of micro media entrepreneurs, and a lack of autonomy when micro media entrepreneurs have to rely on infrastructural platforms over which they have no control. There is a high level of stress and burnout among micro media entrepreneurs, and there is frequent institutional turnover due to the emotional consequences as well as the vulnerability of individual outlets.

The study of micro media industries is important because it calls attention to media projects and platforms that otherwise may be dismissed and trivialized, particularly those that are created for specific minority communities. It helps us to better understand the way that communities with restricted resources can create a thriving media ecology, and gives us insight into how we can better support such endeavors. In this investigation of both media production and reception, we can get a better sense for how media workers and media consumers define what "counts" as a legitimate form of media or media industry, and who participates in shaping these conversations about media values. It also strengthens our understanding of traditional media industries by questioning assumptions about who and what are included within standard definitions, and imagining future possibilities for the way that media industries are changing and will continue to change in the digital era. There is a common fear that media industries are inexorably moving toward conglomeration and consolidation in order to more efficiently make use of economies of scale and scope, and that a smaller number of individuals have come to control an increasingly homogenous media landscape. Indeed, the logics of capitalism combined with our commercial media system have dictated that success for most media corporations is premised on expansion, and as a result we have seen our media landscape become inundated with franchises, sequels and reboots, and transmedia story worlds. But this investigation of micro media industries demonstrates the viability of resistance to this trend. In shedding light on those who are not inter-ested in or are not capable of expansion, we can assess what opportunities for innovation, participation, and diversity exist within these small-scale media formats.

Micro Media Industries

The formations that I call micro media industries are small-scale versions of media production and distribution modeled after traditional forms of mass media whose growth is limited by a number of barriers: namely, they are unable to take advantage of the economies of scale that provide the traditional mech-anism for media sustainability and growth. Micro media industries remain limited in terms of staffing, funding, audience size, and the ability to profit financially in a way that could allow for scaling up. The production team behind such micro media industries can be as limited as one person taking on every role, or up to a handful of individuals that includes largely volunteer and/or temporary participants. The broader category of "micro business" is generally used to describe businesses with one owner and less than five employees, although this designation is often used in the context of accounting and lend-ing. Rather than providing a hard upper limit on the number of staff members who constitute micro media production and distribution, here the designation of "micro" is simply useful in marking a difference from traditional forms of mass media. It seems clear from this investigation of Hmong American media that there are many distinct media entities whose small size, scale, and capac-ity challenge our more standard understanding of media industries.

While the concept of micro media industries is focused on the limited size of those involved in media production and distribution, this scale is of course connected to the limited size of the audience for its products. Indeed, there has long been a trend toward creating media that is targeted toward specific audi-ences, or niche audiences. Yet the emergence of micro media industries is not a product of the same contextual factors that have moved profit logics toward audience fragmentation and narrowcasting—these reflect a desire to market to specific audiences rather than altering the media industries that create prod-ucts for these smaller and smaller populations. There are some instances in which ethnic media is coterminous with niche media, as we can see in exam-ples such as Vietnamese diasporic videos and music that Nhi T. Lieu argues con-stitute a niche media industry in targeting a specific ethnic audience (Lieu 2011). Cases like these reveal the productive overlap between the Hmong micro media industries described here and other similar formations. Yet the term "niche media" is also expansive enough to cover "cable-like" television program-ming like NBC's show *The Slap* or millennially targeted online news outlets like Mic.com that both clearly are produced in a traditional fashion with extensive staff and reach millions of audience members (Lowry 2015). If niche media describes conventional fare that simply aims for a smaller piece of the population, it is clear we need new terms such as "micro media" to describe the distinctively small scale of media production we see in Hmong media.

There are many interrelated concepts that are similar to the formation described here as micro media industries, including "community media," "alternative media," and "citizens' media." Each of these terms can be useful in describing certain aspects of micro media industries—and vice versa, as the concept of micro media industries can help to illuminate and uncover new aspects of these specific media formations. Indeed, these concepts are quite flexible and fluid in circumscribing a wide array of media practices that may be differently understood by different scholars. Yet there are still significant differences between the way these specific terms have been traditionally theorized and the micro media industries analyzed here.

The term "community media" is a broad concept that includes a wide variety of media practices that challenge the norms of mainstream media. Familiar formats encompassed by this term include community radio, community television/video, and community newspapers, although there is a growing trend to also describe various online formations under the umbrella of community media as well. Nevertheless, the primary use for this term is in describing local media with a democratic ethos of being created by and for the people it serves. As such, it is often directly oriented toward informing a geographically circumscribed community about local occurrences or otherwise making a local impact. Community media commonly refers to media institutions whose mandate is service-oriented, rather than primarily being designed to produce financial profit. The mission for community media centers on access and participation— providing media production tools and technologies to local communities, and democratizing the practices of production through involving community members and nonprofessionals (Howley 2005, 16). Some of the other goals may be a commitment to producing and circulating information about local communities, training in media production, building community, or contributing to larger social changes. The funding for such projects can come from a variety of sources, including member contributions, private and public grants, philanthropic relations, and state funding. Yet the overall goal is not to produce profit.

When the profit imperative is bypassed, there are also opportunities for media organizations to foreground political advocacy and challenges to the status quo. These goals are often taken up by "alternative media" outlets, which Downing (2001) further describes with the additional term "radical." Such titles emphasize the political positioning of such media entities as being counter to the mainstream, providing a perspective that is ignored or silenced in more traditional venues. The content may be situated toward protest and dissent, or it may simply eschew professional norms in terms of training, design, aesthetics, editing practices, or the power hierarchies that traditionally govern such media bodies. Similarly, the term "citizens' media" evokes the democratic ideals of encouraging citizens to participate in the public sphere via grassroots media organizations. As Pantelis Vatikiotis (2009) describes, citizens' media practices are a fundamental part of civic culture, as they allow diverse participants to intervene in the political processes constituted through public communication.

All of these terms—community media, alternative media, and citizens' media—may indeed be useful in describing the small-scale forms of media production and distribution taken up within micro media industries. Yet they are not mutually exclusive, and each provides a slightly different valence that emphasizes the unique qualities or differences that pull them apart. For instance, while community media is traditionally centered on local participants, geographically circumscribed regions, and issues of local significance, micro media industries may expand far beyond the local. The Hmong micro media industries examined here are oriented toward diasporic communities positioned all over the globe. Similarly, the political and counterhegemonic orientation of alternative and citizens' media are not necessarily taken up within micro media industries, whose products may more seamlessly align within the commercial or mainstream aesthetics of traditional media industries. There is certainly a political component to any enterprise in which an ethnic minority strives for visibility, self-determination, and participation in a public sphere of their own making. But it would be inaccurate to describe the ethos of all micro media industries as premised on democratizing the processes of media production by transferring control over media to the community, or as oriented toward social justice goals and radical social transformation. It is clear these terms do not fit what we see happening within Hmong American media, and there are many other media outlets that similarly deserve further investigation and more precise categorization.

Hopefully it is already clear by now why the terms "ethnic media" and "diasporic media" are also markedly distinct from what we are seeing within Hmong American micro media industries. Most importantly, this is due to the fact that many forms of ethnic and diasporic media are large-scale ventures that far exceed the limits of "micro," but also because I intend for the category of "micro media" to be useful outside the context of ethnic minority or diasporic communities. As we will see in later discussions and the conclusion, the limits of size and scale are in no way exclusively the purview of ethnically bounded communities and can be seen in any kind of identity formation. This exploration of micro media helps us to challenge the assumption that there are only two kinds of media industries that matter—the massive capitalist conglomerates that have become dominant and the grassroots alternative forms of media that are specifically designed for social justice goals. In examining media projects that occupy a shifting ground in between, we can question this binary split and expand our frameworks around media industries.

The Significance of Size

In order to make sense of what micro media industries do, let us first consider what it is that makes these small-scale media formations "media industries." At a basic level, the Hmong media products described throughout this book consist of similar products that compete in a marketplace and strive for professionalism, like any industry. Gillian Doyle (2013) further defines a media industry in terms of its profit orientation, claiming that for media industries, "the general aim is to make intellectual property, package it and maximize revenues by selling it as many times as is feasible to the widest possible audience and at the highest possible price" (20–21). Such a definition seems premised on the promise of scale, which might exclude smaller ventures facing a set of limits that caps their potential to expand widely. Yet the spirit of this definition is simply that the goal of such ventures is to maximize potential. For small communities, that financial potential might be negligible, but the goal is consistent— despite their size, they still seek to develop the largest possible audience while maintaining financial solvency.

Moreover, amid an intellectual landscape where the term "culture industries" has long been used to refer to the production and distribution of cultural goods and services such as media, it is clear the term "industry" does not always need to refer to a traditional corporate industrial structure. The emergence of the term "creative industries" primarily in the United Kingdom can also be useful in describing new economic models around creative endeavors that "are not vertically integrated industrial silos, but small enterprises, flat-hierarchy, autonomy, risk-taking, project-based work patterns, partnerships and network relations with both clients and competitors" (Hartley and Cunningham 2001, 20). Indeed, using the definition provided here, there are many different media platforms and creative products that could fall within micro media industries that are outside the realm of ethnic or diasporic media. A partial list of possibilities includes blogs, rural newspapers, podcasts, fan-produced media such as fan fiction and fan vids, low-power radio stations, and YouTube channels. The theories advanced in this book are designed to help initiate questions about what might be happening in each of these cases, calling attention to the lively cultures of media production and distribution that risk being dismissed due to their small size. It also builds from the work of Vicki Mayer, Miranda Banks, and John Caldwell (2009) in forwarding production studies as a way of asking how production cultures contribute to social hierarchies and inequalities. In their empirical analyses, they ask how the processes of making media relate to politics, economics, and culture. This specific examination of Hmong American media production and distribution provides a narrow focus for asking questions about how micro media may challenge or redefine how we understand media industries as a whole. It also reveals a number of significant secondary characteristics of micro media industries, including the experiences of micro media entrepreneurs, the rise of hybrid media platforms, opportunities for new participants to have a seat at the table, and missions that go beyond growth, commodification, and capitalization in seeking visibility and community empowerment.

Labor and Entrepreneurship

There are many studies of the way that the content of ethnic media contributes to social factors such as assimilation into mainstream society or engagement with local politics (Gentles-Peart 2014; Tanikella 2009; Viswanath and Arora 2000; Zhou and Cai 2002). But in this examination that foregrounds a media industries perspective and considers these multiskilled media owners as entrepreneurs, it is clear that we must move beyond examining textual content to also consider the labor that produces these texts. Due to the invisibility of micro media industries that are often assumed to be managed by larger, more traditionally sized staffs, this entrepreneurship and its particular meanings often go unrecognized and uninterrogated. Micro media industries clearly deploy a different labor structure from their larger counterparts. This may include a greater dependence on volunteer or temporary workers, a flattening or reworking of traditional labor hierarchies, or single individuals taking up multiple roles. There are also ways in which labor can be obscured or rendered illegible within these small ventures, as entrepreneurs may work to strengthen the company's brand by concealing how few individuals are actually working behind the scenes or what they do. In these cases, audiences can reveal misunderstandings of labor structures through comments such as "the reporter should be fired" or "the photographer should get paid more" when the reality is that there is only one person who takes up all of these roles, and more.

Micro media outlets also may shift our notion of authorship, due to this emphasis on multiskilling over labor differentiation. Traditional forms of mass media have challenged notions of the singular author because production tasks are usually divided up among a collective in order to produce movies, TV shows, comic books, albums, and other media products. This has shaped how we identify and assess media authorship both creatively and technically, as there is an assumption that behind every celebrated auteur is a host of invisible laborers who deserve equal acknowledgment and consideration. Micro media industries have the potential to reemphasize the influence and power of the individual author, reversing these dynamics and aligning the concept of the author more closely with entrepreneurship.

Workers in micro media industries can also reshape how we understand the value of professionalization in these environments. The struggles that micro media entrepreneurs face in gaining media training can help us reframe our understanding of the value that is ascribed to professionalization and its necessity in conferring legitimacy and accountability. They can help to illuminate the complexities of distinguishing between amateur and professional labor, given the flexibility of these terms in the job descriptions of micro media entrepreneurs and their staff.

Hybrid Media Platforms

The technologies that support micro media industries are often substantially different from mainstream media industries and their well-financed counterparts. Micro media entrepreneurs may innovate in the deployment of common technologies, or they may develop altogether new platforms. They also can blur the boundaries between and across media technologies in the creation of hybrid media platforms that challenge what constitutes certain mediums and how we understand their usage. For instance, one of the most popular kinds of Hmong radio is not transmitted via radio waves or received via radio technologies. Rather, what could more accurately be described as Hmong teleconference radio is a form of streaming aural media that is created through setting up a conference call on a computer. This flow of audio content is clearly structured after radio practices, and produces a familiar soundscape that includes news reports, call-in shows, storytelling, and musical performances. Yet it also must be recognized for the way that it challenges the borders of what we might call radio in terms of both technology and the way that users interact with it. Indeed, terms like "radio station owner" or "radio DJ" might be somewhat ill-fitting when describing many of those who are involved with this kind of Hmong radio. Hybrid media platforms do not comfortably fit within a single category or medium, and demand further inquiry into the specific ways that they do and do not align with traditional understandings of what a medium is and does.

The development of hybrid media platforms that challenge our understanding of specific mediums are of course not unique to these Hmong mediums. On the contrary, the boundaries of nearly all forms of media are currently being rewritten due to digital forms of production and distribution in an era of digital convergence. The category of "radio" has long been expanding in order to include digital satellite signals and services such as Sirius and XM, while both terrestrial and online broadcasts are now accessible via streaming mobile apps. There are new formats of streaming audio that are curated algorithmically through platforms such as Spotify or Pandora, while podcasting is opening up new conversations about time-shifted audio content. This investigation provides a number of different examples of Hmong hybrid media platforms and helps us to consider why they are necessary and how they fit into a larger media ecology.

Hmong uses of digital media also point to the possibilities for small communities to tactically engage with the infrastructural possibilities of digital platforms. Lisa Parks (2015) reminds us of the need to read media with "an infrastructural disposition" (357), including considerations of the kinds of physical resources that undergird media but may be difficult to observe or appreciate. For marginalized communities with limited capabilities for developing their own digital infrastructures, this requires attention to the way that components like satellites, cell phones, and radio towers may be deployed in innovative ways by small communities. But we can additionally consider the increasing slippage between infrastructures and platforms, as Jean-Christophe Plantin and Aswin Punathambekar (2019) have argued, due to the massive scale and power of companies like Facebook and Google whose platforms have arguably become infrastructural. This exploration of hybrid media platforms helps us to critique the power disparities engendered by these large-scale digital corporations while also revealing the possibilities for tactical uses of commercial digital platforms that challenge or rework their infrastructural possibilities.

Marginalized Voices

One of the long-standing critiques of traditional media industries is that they are dominated by hegemonic identities and structural barriers that uphold historical exclusions continue to limit diverse participation. Given that micro media industries provide an alternative to mainstream media industries that is defined by low barriers to entry, we can then ask what impact that has had on those with marginalized identities. This includes considerations of how Hmong women, LGBTQ+ people, working class people, people with disabilities, and others are supported or prohibited from various forms of participation in these media outlets. In general, micro media industries are often positioned against the mainstream in terms of pushing back against forces such as commercialization or conglomeration, and certainly face a number of unique challenges. Yet we cannot assume that they are inherently resistant or are invested in a counterhegemonic political identity. Moreover, there are many ways in which the structures of micro media industries are actually prohibitive to new voices, shoring up already existing power dynamics within the community that they serve. Studying these organizations requires sensitivity to the self-determined values and actual political potential of the media that is produced in order to understand the way that micro media industries do or do not increase participation from marginalized citizens or contribute to the silencing of particular perspectives.

Expanding Missions

The mission of micro media industries reflects a wide range of possibilities—some of which include the profit motive of mainstream media and the public service mandate of alternative media, independent media, and community media. But it is unclear what additional possibilities exist for these small organizations, and what impact a potentially unique mandate or mission may have on the production and distribution of content. Given that one of the biggest struggles for small companies is financial solvency, examinations of micro media industries can help to surface new models for overcoming financial barriers. Yet micro media can also help us rethink the push toward capitalization and audience commodification altogether, as there may be alternative structures that become workable for small ventures.

Beyond the question of financial models, Hmong micro media outlets can also help us to reflect on the purposes and functions of diasporic media. While a great deal of research on diasporic and ethnic media explores their role in connecting to the home country and assimilating to the host country, this exploration foregrounds the struggle for Hmong sovereignty through media entrepreneurship. To this end, we see a number of different outcomes that are all achieved through sustained labor and innovation in these media enterprises—including providing a source of information for a community that is starved for it, creating opportunities for self-representation and control over one's own story and narrative, and achieving visibility for a community that is so often neglected and invisible.

This study of Hmong American micro media industries provides a set of case studies that exemplifies the way that digital technologies, platforms, and cultural practices are constantly in motion, evolving in ways that are mutually constitutive. It serves as a reminder that media industries are subject to a set of multiple and contradictory forces. On the one hand, conglomeration has led to massive consolidation of power in the hands of fewer and fewer media corporations—a trend that contributes to further disenfranchisement for minority groups. Yet at the same time, more and more individual media consumers now have the tools and skills to become content producers, software and app designers, self-distributors, and promotional machines. Small communities that previously may not have had the ability to engage in media production and distribution are now finding a seat at the table. This includes those who are politically or socially disempowered, as well as those who have limited access to financial capital and certain kinds of communication technologies.

While small size can certainly play a role in the way that certain media industries evolve and develop, this is not to say that every micro media entity is the same. There are plenty of media outlets across the world that are run by only one person and are nearly indistinguishable from outlets staffed with dozens or even hundreds of workers. Yet there are many cases in which significant differences distinguish organizations of varying size. This investigation of micro media industries asks about the cases when size makes a difference, as in the case for Hmong Americans. Indeed, while the goal of this book is to glean insights into micro media industries more broadly, the cases described here are culturally specific to Hmong Americans. As such, they must be understood through the particular historical contexts of this diasporic population. In order to make sense of the way that their micro media industries have developed, let us more clearly introduce Hmong Americans and their histories.

Who Are Hmong Americans?

People of Hmong ethnicity are believed to have origins in southwestern China, where they were part of a broader Miao ethnic group. In the nineteenth century, many Hmong clans began migrating south to the Indochina peninsula in order to avoid persecution by the Chinese government and to find new land for cultivation. They lived in the mountainous regions of Laos for over one hundred years before the Vietnam War, when the U.S. embassy and Central Intelligence Agency (CIA) began enlisting Hmong men to fight alongside them. Under the leadership of Vang Pao, a major in the Royal Lao Army, a deal was made that the United States would arm the Hmong and help to fight and contain the communist Pathet Lao. In exchange they would gain immediate food and supplies, and it was also believed that the deal included the promise that one day the Hmong would be given a home in the United States (E. Lee 2015, 318). Over 50,000 Hmong were recruited to join as allies in what was known as the Secret War, since the United States was publicly stating that they were only doing humanitarian work in Laos and concealed their use of Hmong fighters. In reality, approximately 17,000 Hmong died during the Vietnam conflict, and when the United States pulled out of the region in 1975 the remaining families were left fighting for their lives. Some families were airlifted out of the region, but many thousands more fled into the jungles or out of Laos, making the dangerous trek across the Mekong River into Thailand. Nearly 100,000 Hmong arrived in northeastern Thailand and began settling into refugee camps such as Ban Vinai, Nam Phong, and Nong Khai. From there, they began migrating to countries around the world that opened to accept Hmong refugees.

Although the world's largest populations of Hmong are still in Asia—with around three million in China and one million in northern Vietnam—this history of conflict in Laos reveals the roots of the post-1975 Hmong global diaspora. It resulted in populations of Hmong in the United States, Canada, French Guyana, France, Australia, and a few other countries. The United States has the largest community of diasporic Hmong at around 260,000 as of the 2010 U.S. Census. This includes a population of around 91,000 throughout central California, with large populations in Sacramento, Merced, and Fresno. The Twin Cities are home to the densest concentration of Hmong, with around 66,000 in the Minneapolis–St. Paul metro area. Wisconsin has a number of smaller Hmong communities spread throughout the state, totaling around

50,000 when aggregated. These patterns of settlement are due to a number of factors, including the location of the nongovernmental agencies who agree to sponsor incoming refugees, the resources available through social service agencies in the area, and the existence of other family and community in the area. Hmong Americans have also undergone significant secondary migration in the years following their initial settlement, making their own choices about the cities and communities they wanted to call home.

As members of the 1.2 million refugees from Vietnam, Cambodia, and Laos as a result of the Vietnam War, Hmong Americans have been "set decidedly outside the model minority" (E. Lee 2015, 334). The term "model minority" refers to the long-standing stereotype that Asian American immigrants to the United States are disproportionately successful in terms of educational attainment, family income, home ownership, and a number of other factors. This framework works to uphold white supremacy, as it uses efforts to assimilate this minority group as docile and productive citizens to comparatively denigrate Black and Brown racialized communities. Indeed, it is a historical fact that the Immigration and Nationality Act of 1965 lifted a decades-old prohibition on immigration from Asia to open the door for highly skilled and educated laborers. This created an influx of immigrants from India, Korea, and China who were able to work in tech, health care, and higher education. In contrast, when Hmong refugees arrived in the United States with limited language skills or job proficiencies, they struggled to find employment and many families relied on welfare assistance. The 1990 U.S. Census reported that 60 percent of Hmong were unemployed, and that the rate of Hmong working in manufacturing jobs was double the national average (Vang 2012). While Hmong communities have made tremendous strides in closing these gaps by moving off welfare programs and lowering rates of unemployment and poverty, there are still inequities. Reports from the 2010 U.S. Census reveal that Hmong family incomes were $15,000 lower than the total U.S. population ($47,400 as compared to $62,100) (Vang 2013).

These facts are not meant to show Hmong as lacking in any way. On the contrary, Chia Youyee Vang cautions that although resettlement brought the loss of self-sufficiency for many Hmong in the United States, we should not overlook the opportunities it afforded in terms of education, employment, and business opportunities (Vang 2010, 32). Thousands of Hmong Americans are earning college degrees, becoming political leaders in their communities, opening successful businesses, and participating in all facets of American society. Yet these data serve to challenge the accuracy of the model minority framework and position Hmong Americans within the larger racialized context in which so many Asian immigrant communities continue to be understood. It is clear that the Asian American community encompassed by this category is extremely heterogeneous and includes immigrant families whose story does not align with these supposedly "model" characteristics. One of the political projects of Asian American studies has been to uncover and highlight the struggles that many Asian American communities continue to face. Hmong Americans are certainly among those who are systemically left out of Asian American imaginaries, along with their specific struggles.

Understanding Hmong Media

The idea that Hmong Americans are positioned adjacent to, rather than within, the collective known as Asian America is also reflected in studies of Asian American media use. Research focused on Asian American media use consistently relies on only the six largest ethnic groups (Chinese, Indian, Filipino, Vietnamese, Korean, and Japanese) when sampling Asian American populations. Given that Hmong are the ninth-largest ethnic Asian population in the United States, it is nearly impossible to find empirical data on Hmong American consumer habits, access to technologies, or media use. It can generally be assumed that when media studies scholars describe the practices of Asian Americans, they are not able to disaggregate Hmong Americans from their data set in order to contribute any insights about this specific community.

Researchers from the interdisciplinary formation of Hmong American studies have produced some work on Hmong media use, often from a sociological or anthropological perspective. These studies have largely centered on the role of Hmong video production in upholding dominant narratives about Hmong identities, subjectivities, and histories (Koltyk 1993; G. Y. Lee 2006; Schein 2004). Investigations of home videos, commercial videos, and documentaries reveal the important role videos have played in preserving narratives of Hmong history, inspiring pride for Hmong culture and identification across national borders, and evoking longing for the homeland. Mitch Ogden (2015) analyzes VHS videocassettes alongside audio cassette tapes, arguing that both forms of what he terms "magnetic media" have been used by Hmong families across the diaspora to imagine different forms of the homeland in manifesting images of Laos, China, and a utopian homeland of their own imagining. In Louisa Schein's extensive research on Hmong video cultures, she argues that Hmong video practices cannot be extricated from ideologies of gender and sexuality. Many of the videos that Hmong American men have created about the homeland rely on Orientalist images of Asian femininity as sexualized and exotic, and produce longing for a Hmong femininity that is subordinated to Hmong men (Schein 2004). Video creation has also played a more direct political role for Hmong Americans, who may have learned to connect the oppression of Hmong peoples to the need to fight for a Hmong nation-state (Baird 2014). Beyond these studies of VHS and DVD videos, scholars have also examined Hmong videos shared on YouTube. Yet even within a digitally mediated realm, the videos shared online play a similar role in terms of culture and politics—serving to facilitate the creation of a pan-Hmong identity for Hmong spread across the world, which can collapse or elide differences between the experiences of Hmong in the United States versus Hmong in Asia (Falk 2013; Yang 2008).

The self-representations and narratives found within Hmong videos serve as a necessary foil to the complete absence of Hmong Americans within mainstream media representations. As a minority within the already minoritized category of Asian Americans, Hmong Americans are rarely discussed in news media, and Hmong characters are rarely identified in fictional narratives on film and television. The Clint Eastwood movie *Gran Torino* (2008) remains one of the only Hollywood movies to feature Hmong Americans. Eastwood stars as Walt Kowalski, a grumpy Korean War vet who comes to befriend and rescue his Hmong American neighbors from gang violence. The movie proved extremely controversial in Hmong American communities, who responded with complaints about inaccurate cultural representations, a frustrating reliance on stereotypes, and failure to truly give agency to its Hmong actors (Schein and Thoj 2009). Hmong activists have also routinely condemned news coverage of their communities in cities like Eau Claire, Wisconsin, and St. Paul, Minnesota. They assert that the only stories about Hmong Americans center on sensationalized tragedies such as when Hmong hunters are involved in violent crime, both as perpetrators and victims. Scholars have affirmed that these news stories uphold harmful stereotypes of Hmong culture as primitive and violent (Baldillo, Mendy, and Eng 2005; Fung 2015).

Such work productively identifies the ways that Hmong videos and mainstream imagery are connected to the construction of Hmong American identities. Yet there has been little research on many other forms of Hmong American media, such as radio, newspapers, or television stations. Another gap in the literature on Hmong media exists with regard to the media practices of second-generation Hmong Americans who are immersed in the context of mainstream American media. Gary Yia Lee (2006) states that second-generation Hmong immigrants are "much more assimilated into the local cultures and languages of the new host countries where they have grown up, . . . [and thus they] show little interest in Hmong videos or cultural traditions, and . . . have a very different attitude to the homeland of their parents" (2–3). While it is certainly the case that younger generations of Hmong have different attitudes from their parents, in interviews conducted for this research I have found that many college-aged students remain interested in Hmong media as a way of connecting to their cultural heritage. Their assimilation to the mainstream culture in the United States makes their sustained interest in Hmong media and culture even more important to investigate and understand, particularly in the ways that it plays an important role in shaping the future of what Hmong media will look like and what function it will serve.

This study also seeks to remedy the combined dearth of research in both the media practices of younger Hmong generations and Hmong digital practices more generally, which are in need of deeper investigation. Nicholas Tapp's study from 2000 points to the Hmong Electronic Resources Project as a repository of Hmong cyberactivity, listing the websites of Hmong organizations, commercial sites promoting Hmong CDs, and sites offering digital versions of Hmong journals, books, and educational materials about Hmong culture. This catalog of Hmong digital activity remains at the level of what we might call "Web 1.0," which largely relies on static, unidirectional websites where internet users can passively consume information but does not allow for interactivity or user-generated content (Cormode and Krishnamurthy 2008). Faith Nibbs (2016) has expanded this scholarship with her investigation of Hmong women's use of social networking software, arguing that platforms such as Facebook and YouTube allow Hmong women to challenge and renegotiate gendered power relations in their communities. She notes that communication on these web forums can be agentic and empowering, opening up far-reaching avenues for dialogue that challenges the gendered power hierarchies of their everyday lives. Yet there is clearly more need for research on the widespread use of social media and Web 2.0 by Hmong across the diaspora.

Asian American Digital Divides

These concerns about diversifying our understanding of Hmong digital media use are also connected to a need for more research probing the assumption that Asian Americans are disproportionately wired (Balance 2012; Nakamura 2005; Pew Research Center 2011). As a 2013 report from Nielsen stated, "Asian Americans are digital pioneers, adopting technology faster than any other segment. With higher rates of smartphone usage, online video consumption, and internet connectivity, they are redefining the way they watch, listen, and interact" (Nielsen 2013). But just as the study of specific Asian American communities can help to debunk the homogenizing myth of the model minority, studies of specific instances of Asian American digital media usage are necessary in countering assumptions about what we might consider the "digital model minority." Many Hmong Americans do not have equitable access to or use of information technologies or digital tools, and Hmong American digital participation must be contextualized through the intertwined factors of low socioeconomic status, and low English fluency and literacy. Although these factors certainly do not determine the technological usage of Hmong Americans, these factors can provide persistent barriers that must be overcome, as accords with many discussions of the digital divide.

Early studies of the "digital divide" largely focused on questions of access to computers, the internet, mobile phones, and other communication technologies.

Yet this simple binary of "haves" and "have nots" obscures the richness and complexities of the different ways that people actually interact with digital technologies (Warschauer 2003). Moreover, this logic seems to naively imply that simply gifting computers or internet access to otherwise impoverished communities would necessarily improve their conditions—an assumption that has led to the creation of countless pieces of legislation designed to increase access without accompanying plans for education, development of infrastructure, or culturally specific modes of integration. To combat these deficiencies, scholars are now focusing on richer dimensions of digital life, such as ownership, participation, creation, and new media literacy. In trying to make sense of where Hmong Americans fall within this portrait of digital life, we must move beyond basic assumptions about certain demographic categories in order to more accurately understand how communications technologies and digital media fit into the everyday lives of Hmong Americans.

When talking to Hmong community members about how they access information, many openly affirmed that they considered "word of mouth" to be the primary way that they learned about what is going on in the Hmong community. Professionals who specifically worked in the Hmong community—including community organizers, health care professionals, and community leaders—also stated that they did not see Hmong media as a reliable way for communicating a message to their local communities. Rather, if they needed to inform Hmong folks about an upcoming event or other issue of importance, they routinely knocked on doors or made phone calls to spread the message. Studies of Hmong health interventions also provide insight into Hmong communication patterns, as those working in the arena of health communication are always working to reach populations as efficiently and effectively as possible. The literature on Hmong health communication reveals a similar pattern— when working to communicate with Hmong communities about an issue such as disease prevention or improving a community's health literacy, Hmong media is never mentioned. Instead, messages about health are customarily communicated through face-to-face programming such as workshops and training programs (Depke and Onitilo 2011; Kagawa-Singer et al. 2009; Sparks 2014). Moreover, studies of Hmong health interventions often make the claim that health information needs to be communicated in a top-down fashion that begins with Hmong elders and community leaders, rather than creating a form of communication that is equally available or accessible to all members of the community at once such as mass media (Schroepfer et al. 2010).

This book focuses on Hmong mass media and social media in order to illuminate the wide varieties of uses and meanings for each format, as well as the active role that Hmong Americans are playing in developing media organizations. In centering stories of agency, this investigation contrasts with the portrayals of Hmong as victims who are powerless in shaping their own circumstances. Chia Youyee Vang (2010) reminds us that Hmong Americans and other immigrants "are not only changed by the new society but also contribute to the dynamic communities in which they settle" (4). The same can be said of relations to media technologies and cultures—that the technologies themselves are shaped by those who use them, including the culturally specific ways that Hmong Americans utilize various forms of communication.

Of course this does not mean that the possibilities are limitless or that communication technologies serve only to empower and transform. On the contrary, there are also numerous ways in which Hmong American media cultures reveal the limits and struggles they face. But rather than becoming mired in binaries of digital optimism versus digital pessimism, this research is premised on the understanding that digital technologies are taken up in ambivalent ways. Whitney Phillips and Ryan Milner (2017) remind us that there are no simple, one-size-fits-all ways of understanding digital media due to the diversity of users and their motivations. Their scholarship reminds us that media cultures can be simultaneously helpful and harmful, rather than manifesting only one kind of impact. In the same way, Hmong American mass media and social media can be studied for the unique contributions and insights revealed within their industrial formations without needing to decide whether they should be celebrated or condemned.

Beyond teaching us about Hmong media, the stories in this book more generally provide a small glimpse into contemporary Hmong American life and culture. While the field of Hmong studies is flourishing and scholars continue to produce insights on the specific nuances of this population, it remains a relatively small field of study with limited book-length forays into specific aspects of contemporary Hmong American culture. As such, this book is intended to provide an examination of Hmong media cultures as one way of showing the breadth and depth of Hmong American experiences, broadening beyond simplistic or essentializing renderings of this heterogeneous population. As a media studies scholar, I know well the threat posed by the burden of representation—that is, the notion that when there are too few representations of a minority group, those few representations matter more and are subject to closer scrutiny. Given that I am not Hmong American myself, there are clearly limits to my understanding of Hmong American cultures. Yet I strive to highlight the voices of Hmong Americans throughout this book, and enrich this investigation of media cultures by casting light on the experiences of those of varying age, generation, gender identity, sexual orientation, class background, geographic region, and occupation.

Researching Hmong Media Industries, 2012–2018

The process of investigating Hmong American media for this book spanned many years and took many forms. After moving to Madison, Wisconsin, in

2012, I began familiarizing myself with local Hmong communities and organizations so that I could learn more about what kind of media was being produced and consumed by Hmong Americans. My research took me to many cities with sizable Hmong populations, including Appleton, Green Bay, and Milwaukee in Wisconsin, as well as Fresno, California, and St. Paul, Minnesota. In each location, I visited sites where media production took place and conducted interviews with fifty individuals who worked in Hmong media industries—including radio DJs and station owners, television network owners and executives, print and broadcast journalists, photographers, musicians, YouTubers, podcasters, bloggers, software engineers, app developers, and social media influencers.[1] Since one of the goals of this project is to document and call attention to the enormous work these community leaders are doing through creating Hmong American media, throughout this book I identify Hmong media producers by name and strive to record their histories as directly as possible.

In addition to conversations with media producers and professionals, I conducted forty-eight interviews with everyday Hmong American consumers and audience members.[2] When describing or quoting from these private citizens, I use pseudonymous first names and protect their anonymity. These interviews were conducted in English if the participant was comfortable with English, or through an interpreter if they preferred to speak in Hmong. Participants initially included Hmong American college students who were recruited through Hmong language courses and student organizations, Hmong elders who spent time gathering in community centers, and people I met through attending Hmong events. From there, additional participants were recruited via word of mouth and through the personal networks of my research assistants, colleagues, and interpreters. The majority of our conversations were straightforward interviews in which participants were asked to describe what kind of media they consumed and what it meant to them. But when possible, I conducted more in-depth interviews that took place in individual homes, where participants were invited to actually demonstrate the way that they interacted with media. This included showing how they used various apps on their cell phones and tablets, how they called into teleconference radio programs, what channels they liked to watch on the television, and what websites or software they knew how to use on their computers and laptops. These demonstrations of the different ways that participants interacted with technology in their homes offered a more naturalistic and nuanced perspective of their relationships with media than could be ascertained through oral responses to questions.

Discussions about media consumption were supplemented with analysis of the content of Hmong media texts, including radio broadcasts, television programs, movies, and newspapers. Since the majority of these texts were in Hmong language, I enlisted the help of many bilingual Hmong American research assistants—in total, nine undergraduates and two graduate students from 2013 to 2015. Together they translated hundreds of hours of Hmong radio programs, videos, and television programs into English transcripts. In 2015, a core group of five Hmong American research assistants also met up with me on a weekly basis to discuss media texts in depth so that we could layer cultural meaning onto the direct English translations they had produced. This allowed an opportunity to explain the nuances of certain Hmong phrases that were particularly difficult to translate directly into English (for instance, what was translated as the word "frightened" might more accurately be explained as a superstitious fear of losing part of your soul), as well as to annotate translations with more detail (for instance, if the speaker was laughing, did that laughter seem to actually connote that the statement was funny, or was it more of a nervous or awkward laugh?). We also spent many hours using the media scripts as a launching pad for lively, free-flowing discussions of contemporary Hmong cultural debates around topics like marriage and courtship customs, medicine and health, shamanism and Christianity, education, parental expectations, gender roles, family structures, and more. In this sense, our weekly group discussions can be seen to serve some of the same functions of a focus group—centering the voices of multiple Hmong Americans as they collectively debated the meaning of media texts and how certain texts connected to Hmong culture and life.

While the body of texts recorded, documented, and assessed over the course of this research comprise a meaningful archive, it is important to note that my goal in this book is not to produce a rigorous textual analysis of any particular Hmong media. The sampling methods used were sporadic and did not strive to be representative in any sense; I simply told my research assistants to tune into Hmong media when they had available time and when the content seemed interesting to them. We attempted to gather recordings from a wide variety of programs and formats, but if one show led to particularly rich discussions, we would stick with it for a bit longer. The goal was simply to gain familiarity with the wide range of Hmong media texts and to be able to triangulate insights from interviews alongside actual media texts.

I also have used pedagogy as a way of facilitating conversations about Hmong media and increasing Hmong media capacity, teaching workshops on digital storytelling to Hmong youth, helping a Hmong American nonprofit develop skills in media production and strategic communication, and teaching a course for Hmong college students on preserving Hmong women's stories through oral history and documentary film. These activities were particularly important to me because they allowed me a small form of giving back to the community that gave so much to me throughout this research project. During the portion of interviews where I asked interviewees if they had any questions for me, it was typical for older Hmong participants to straightforwardly ask me, "How will your research help Hmong people?" This question is rooted in a number of different concerns, but one of the realities is that Hmong people have a long history of being objects of study by outsiders and feeling exploited by the process. As in all academic research, it is important to recognize the power dynamic wherein participants may gain nothing from being studied, while the researcher receives a number of individual career benefits. In a town dominated by a research university like the University of Wisconsin–Madison, the local residents are often oversampled by eager researchers—and this was certainly the case for Hmong Americans in Madison, who sometimes told me they had already participated in too many studies. One of my informants warned me that she knew some Hmong families who had been hurt by researchers who demanded much of their time and personal information, and then disappeared without ever coming back to tell them what happened to the research. There is also the issue that many Hmong I talked to were concerned about being portrayed in a positive light, rather than being criticized or having the community's "dirty laundry" aired in public. Indeed, there are many issues Hmong American communities are facing—including practices of polygamy, sexual and domestic violence, abusive international marriage, underage marriage, and others—that some wanted to avoid discussing with outsiders.

For those who were interested in participating, I tried to explain that my research would end up in a book that college students could read in their classes, which would help Hmong people because otherwise their stories and experiences might be overlooked. But I was always seeking to develop new ways that my research could actually give back to the Hmong community. This was why I worked to develop these pedagogical programs and volunteered for nonprofit organizations that served Hmong American communities. I also participated in interviews with Hmong American mass media outlets so that I could strive to share my research questions and findings in a way that was legible to a broader Hmong community, rather than solely focusing on academic publications. This issue is very important to me, and I am constantly seeking improvement and new perspectives on how researchers can build more productive relationships with the communities they study.

Outline of Book Chapters

This story begins by exploring the Hmong American newspaper industry. Chapter 2 considers the way that the traditional form of print media is dominated by outlets with extremely small staffs and uses this case to explore how micro media industries operate more generally. This includes reframing conversations about Hmong newspaper owners as entrepreneurs so that we can more clearly locate the impact of innovation on their labor. Indeed, these outlets that are often assumed to represent the efforts of a collective newsroom or a multilayered news organization must be reframed as the project of individuals with an extremely broad skill set. It asks how micro media news entrepreneurs, in the absence of a robust community of practice among professional colleagues, build community with their audience as evidenced through letters to the editor. This chapter also helps to position single media entities such as newspapers within the larger interconnected Hmong media ecology.

Chapter 3 continues this conversation about the production of Hmong news and journalism, but turns to the audiovisual realm of video or television news. This includes discussion of one of the very few Hmong American terrestrial television stations, Hmong TV Network. This station is able to overcome the financial challenges of participating in the advertiser-supported medium of television, but also struggles with its limited staff to engage in the production of narrative television programming. In its efforts to reach a broad Hmong audience, Hmong TV Network posts its news broadcasts to a YouTube channel, where it becomes indistinguishable from the news programs posted by a number of other Hmong video news outlets such as 3HMONGtv, Hmong TV 24 Hours, and Suab Hmong News. Yet in contrast to Hmong TV Network, these other popular video news outlets live only online and must be considered a hybrid media platform that expands our understanding of "television." In an online environment, these television channels come to rely on YouTube's algorithms to create televisual flow. They also open themselves up to more immediate forms of feedback and criticism, as we see in an incident with Hmong TV 24 Hours in which audiences were outraged by one of the station's videos. We see that micro media entrepreneurs may fight for legitimacy and professionalism through emulating the look of traditional media, but that the online environment allows opportunities for participation that reveal new avenues for gaining media power.

These themes of contestations over media power and the potential offered by hybrid media platforms are continued in chapter 4, which examines Hmong radio industries. This includes an exploration of the different ways Hmong radio outlets have developed in the more traditional formats of community radio, AM/FM stations, and low-power stations. But it focuses primarily on an innovative form of Hmong radio based on teleconference calls that are accessed through cell phones. These teleconference radio programs are noteworthy for their technological novelty, but also because it is primarily Hmong American women who own them and facilitate conversations as DJs and hosts. This woman-centered participatory format allows for a wide variety of discourses to flourish, but it has also suffered from gendered discourses of value that have worked to delegitimize and downplay its deep cultural impact.

Chapter 5 continues this project of centering women-led media outlets in its examination of queer Hmong American audio programs. This includes a radio show called *Nplooj*, a podcast called *Hoochim*, and a radio series called

Poj Laib / Bad Hmong Girl. These largely English-language programs explore the nuances of Hmong American gender and sexuality, provide support for many vulnerable populations, and challenge the heteronormativity and patriarchal norms of the more mainstream Hmong media landscape. They provide a critique of what they feel is a singular narrative of Hmongness that is upheld by Hmong micro media industries, and develop new forms of audio culture for sustained resistance.

Chapter 6 examines social media producers who participate on a number of different platforms, including YouTube, Twitter, Instagram, and personal blogs. These Hmong micro-celebrities fall within the large category of independent professionals who benefit from producing a body of media texts that turns themselves into commodities. In considering the differences between micro media entrepreneurs who put forward a professional organizational identity and those who foreground an authentic personal identity, we can understand some of the ways in which neoliberal forces are shaping the options available to media entrepreneurs with limited resources. I then conclude with a chapter that explores some examples of micro media industries from outside the Hmong American media ecology, pointing to the broader applicability of this research and the dynamics of micro media industries as a way of strengthening our understanding of all components of the media landscape.

By the time my research on this topic has concluded, I predict that many Hmong micro media outlets will have risen, buoyed by a groundswell of optimism, passion, and the desire to connect with others. And Hmong micro media outlets will have collapsed, defeated by the accumulation of exhaustion, financial insolvency, personal life changes facing the individual at the helm, and shifting audience demands and desires. In the years that I have studied Hmong media industries, this has certainly been the case. This is not to say that the mainstream media landscape is any less volatile; network television pilot season is a breeding ground for precarious media labor, and throngs of nonunionized film crews are required to work project by project. Yet when only one person has the power to shape successes and failures, the potential is that much greater for rapid change. Whatever the fate of the outlets examined here, it is my hope that this snapshot of a moment in time for Hmong American media offers important insights across the field of media studies as outlets of all sizes adapt to changes in the media landscape.

2

Without a Newsroom
• •
Journalism and the Micro
Media Empire

When I run into Wameng Moua at a Hmong American arts festival in St. Paul, his arms are full of newspapers. He is excited to show me the latest issue of *Hmong Today*, the newspaper he has run since 2005. "I've been building up the paper, it's way better than it was two or three years ago," he says. As he flips through the pages, he begins to reveal some conflicted feelings about how the newspaper has changed. One the one hand, the pages are gorgeously designed and overflowing with his artful photography. He is proud of the increased number of advertisements he has been able to secure, since he relies on advertising dollars to support the production of his free community newspaper. But on the other hand, he is also somewhat disappointed because this shift toward a graphic-heavy design reflects a capitulation to audiences who have grown so accustomed to social media posts they are no longer as interested in his lengthy investigative articles. "Now we have very few words, a lot of pictures," he says. "That's why *Hmong Today* gets picked up, people wanna see themselves or people they know. We've gone picture-heavy, but it's popular. I'm just doing what people want."

These conflicts over changing expectations for news media in response to the rise of digital media have impacted the entire U.S. newspaper industry. Many mainstream news organizations are in a state of decline due to a reliance on outdated business models and the ubiquity of new media technologies that have changed the way that readers consume and engage with media content (Siles and Boczkowski 2012). Although the professional role of the fourth estate in producing reliable and objective reporting on issues of local, national, and global significance is as important as ever, the popularity of social media and Web 2.0 have also brought increased expectations that readers can access information immediately, and for free. The newspapers that have survived have responded by dramatically reducing their staffs and restructuring their workforce, as well as reassessing their core values to center reader relationships and participation (Usher 2014).

But in many ways, these struggles and shifts have brought mainstream newspapers closer to the way that ethnic newspapers have always been produced. Newspapers that are made by and for ethnic minority communities also struggle and are limited by factors such as financial resources, audience size, and the need to adapt to new technologies. While advertisers are increasingly losing interest in buying ad space in mainstream publications, they have always been skeptical of outlets that target small niche audiences. Ethnic media have been forced to make do amid considerable instability, often sustaining production despite enormous financial struggles because they are so committed to their mission. This includes goals such as maintaining a sense of identity and community in diaspora, helping immigrants adapt to their new surroundings, and educating about what is happening locally and in the home country. There are certainly exemplars of ethnic media that are well staffed and highly profitable, including a number of Spanish-language and Chinese-language ethnic media outlets in the United States whose existence affirms that "ethnic media" is not synonymous with "micro media." Yet as Lin and Song (2006) discovered, the majority of ethnic media are "small, community-based mom-and-pop businesses" (373).

This is certainly the case for the Hmong American newspaper industry, which is composed entirely of extremely small enterprises staffed with only a handful of volunteers. At these newspapers, only one person is responsible for multiple aspects of production—such as making assignments, writing articles, taking photographs, editing content, handling advertisements, crafting layouts, printing, and distributing. Wameng Moua describes the staff of *Hmong Today* as compared to a mainstream publication: "When you walk into other newspapers you have a guy who sells ads, a guy who does the photography, an editor. I'm like, yeah, I do all that by myself. I wear all the hats. We don't have a budget to hire these positions, we're constrained by what we have. When there's a story to cover, I'm the guy who calls, I'm the guy who makes arrangements, I show up to take pictures, write the article, edit it, publish it. Every single little thing." When we look at the pages of an issue together and he describes all the work that he has put into a single issue, it is clear that his responsibilities cover a lot of ground—including the fact that he is also the one responsible for delivering the papers to local events. It seems inappropriate to view these kinds of micro media news organizations as simply smaller, understaffed versions of a larger news organization. Their output may look similar to a newspaper produced by a large professional staff, but what is happening behind the scenes is distinct and deserving of examination. We might ask if the concept of a "newsroom" is still functional when there are only one or two individuals comprising the entire "news organization." Understanding the way these small news organizations operate can also help us to reconsider many of the shifting dynamics of contemporary mainstream news organizations—including the move toward small flexible teams with flattened power hierarchies, the use of so-called one-man-band journalism, the place of bloggers and participatory journalism, and a number of other innovations.

This chapter conducts an industrial analysis of Hmong American newspapers, examining the impact of their small labor force on a variety of factors—including business management, production, distribution, content, professional identity formations, and audience engagement. It takes up the call by Amanda Lotz (2009) to conduct industry-level media studies that assess the macro-level industrial landscape alongside the micro-level data gained from studying specific workplaces and communities. In doing so, we can better understand what it means that Hmong newspapers comprise a micro media industry—both for the individual at the helm and the broader community they serve. It begins with a description of the broad contours of the Hmong news landscape and the rise of key publications. It then closely examines two papers in particular—*Hmong Today* and the *Hmong Tribune*—synthesizing interviews with their two founders alongside textual analyses of the newspapers themselves.

In positioning these micro-staffed news outlets within the larger Hmong media ecology, we will see why it is important to understand the individuals who run micro media outlets as entrepreneurs, rather than simply journalists. I argue that their survival and resilience amid immense resource scarcity has been predicated on a number of different innovations—including the entrepreneurialism of creating a multimedia empire that extends far beyond an individual newspaper, developing multiple skills to alleviate the need for large staffs, and expanding their professional community of practice beyond the newsroom. Yet they also face tremendous limitations and challenges in doing so, including the potential for burnout and the vulnerability of each outlet. Their need to go it alone also leads to complicated relationships with their audience, as we can see in the opening story about Wameng Moua and the way he negotiated his professional duties in relation to his small audience. Unlike community or participatory media that focus primarily on democratizing media production, these micro-staffed newspapers are not necessarily premised on increasing participation from Hmong American community members. Yet readers and consumers still play an important role in providing feedback to micro media entrepreneurs who are lacking a professional community. These insights help us to see what it takes to create a thriving micro media ecology, as well as providing a cautionary tale about some of the risks and limitations. Together they help to break down larger assumptions about changes in the media landscape and what they can mean for communication within marginalized ethnic communities.

Understanding Small Journalism

One of the many contributing factors to the journalism crisis has been the rise of media conglomeration, where large publishing companies like Gannett, the McClatchy Company, and Tronc have acquired dozens of smaller newspapers. The consequences for media mergers are dire on a number of fronts, leading to feelings of alienation among workers, a decrease in journalists' ability to adequately cover local news, and impaired attempts to diversify newsrooms. Peter Gade (2004) examined the impact of shrinking newsroom staffs from an organizational development perspective, assessing the success of implementing newsroom changes on morale. He found that these changes led to a decrease in morale because news values have been supplanted by profit-driven business values, and overall the rank-and-file journalists felt less productive and efficient in the newsroom.

In response to shrinking newsrooms, many television news organizations have increasingly begun to rely on extremely small mobile teams. In fact, it is not uncommon within video news for one person to write, shoot, and edit their own packages—a practice known by many names, including mobile journalism, the one-man band, video journalism, solo journalism, and backpack journalism. Newsrooms that deploy this kind of journalism decrease their horizontal complexity as they shift their labor practices toward multiskilling, where individuals take on a wide array of different professional tasks rather than specializing (Wallace 2009). Multiskilled field operators have some strengths, such as being able to maintain direct control over their professional output and learning every aspect of the job in a short amount of time. Yet those who belong to more traditional news crews with labor differentiation feel more competent in specialized aspects of their profession and that they can respond more confidently during moments of uncertainty (Blankenship 2016).

While these changes have deeply reformed the entire news industry, fears about widespread media conglomeration have also been countered by the reality that small news outlets have remained strong and resilient. In 2017, nearly 97 percent of the regularly published newspapers in the United States (6,851 out of 7,071) had circulations smaller than 50,000 (Radcliffe and Ali 2017). This includes many rural news outlets whose mission is to cover geographic areas that extend far beyond urban centers (Baines 2012), as well as what Metzgar, Kurpius, and Rowley (2011) define as hyperlocal media—"geographically-based, community-oriented, original-news-reporting organizations indigenous to the web and intended to fill perceived gaps in coverage of an issue or region and to promote civic engagement" (774). Scholarship on these small outlets has primarily focused on two issues—the significance of local news, and the adaptation of small outlets to digital technologies. They reveal that it is possible for these small outlets to be successful if they are closely attuned to the specific dynamics and contexts of their location (Hess and Waller 2014; Schultz and Jones 2017).

The existence of these smaller news outlets tells us that Hmong American newspapers are not the only outlets that have remained focused on a limited audience amid wider changes in the journalism landscape. Yet within these studies of rural and hyperlocal news outlets, it is unclear what size staff they actually employ. The designation of small circulation refers to the size of audience, not the number of employees, and the studies referenced here do not focus on issues of labor. Moreover, much of this scholarship on adaptations to new media are interested in recent developments, when the reality is that micro media industries such as Hmong American newspapers have operated in this fashion since their inception. This chapter maps out the history of micro media industries that began long before the rise of digital media, and assesses the impact of relying on a small number of workers as well as the struggles that media entrepreneurs face when this is their only viable option.

The Rise of Hmong American Newspapers

The earliest reports of Hmong American newspapers date to the mid-1980s, when the *Hmong Chronicle* could be found on the news racks in Fresno. Six months into its printing, Ben Vue and two partners took it over with the goal of growing the readership. But after only one year they ended up selling the printing equipment and shutting the paper down (N. Xiong 2001). In 1998, Steve Thao started up the *Hmong Tribune* in St. Paul, Minnesota. The *Tribune* was printed monthly for the first two years, but then started to struggle. In the November 1999 issue, Thao wrote a message on the editorial page with an open call for a young person who could take over as editor in chief. He stated, "As I am still single and without any family or large financial obligations I can do this newspaper . . . [but] my full time work in another capacity has taken much all of my time" (S. Thao 1999). The masthead of the newspaper included between eight and twelve contributors and staff writers, but Thao's name was included as the publisher-editor and managing editor, as well as under staff writer and photographer. Thao continued printing the paper intermittently until 2016, when he felt that social media had taken the place of print news and stopped printing altogether.

The most reliable Hmong newspapers in the United States have been the *Hmong Times* and *Hmong Today*, both of which are produced in Minnesota. The *Hmong Times* was started by Dick Wetzler, a white man who started becoming involved with the Hmong community in 1995 through his job teaching math at a community college in St. Paul. Not only was he the advisor for the students' Asian club, but he helped Hmong members at his church and owned an apartment building whose tenants were primarily Hmong. Together with a former student, Wetzler first created a Hmong directory that listed all the Hmong businesses and families with Hmong surnames in Minnesota. By 1998, internet searches and unlisted cell phone numbers had obviated the need for a Hmong yellow pages, and he turned his attention to starting a Hmong newspaper called the *Hmong Times* along with a Hmong partner named Cheu Lee. Although the two did not have much experience in journalism, they recognized the need for a Hmong news outlet in Minnesota. Its issues came out every other month, and they were delivered to 650 locations in St. Paul. As of 2018 they are still printing regularly; their print circulation is listed at approximately 16,000, and stories are published simultaneously on the newspaper's website. Cheu Lee parted ways with the *Hmong Times* in 2000 and founded his own monthly newspaper called *Hmong Pages* in 2010.

Hmong Today was founded in 2005 by Wameng Moua, along with his wife Zeng Vang, who is a graphic designer. At that time, he noticed that there was a lot of interest in the Hmong American community due to the influx of Hmong refugees to the Twin Cities area, as well as a high-profile criminal case in Wisconsin involving a Hmong hunter. He knew that the Hmong newspaper business was risky, having seen a number of other newspapers and magazines fail after only a handful of issues. But Moua threw himself into the project, taking on nearly all the writing, photography, and editing. He has worked with a number of writers over the years, but given the high turnover he ends up taking on the lion's share of labor himself. The paper is part of a coalition with other ethnic media called the Minnesota Multicultural Media Consortium. Their membership in this consortium helps to bolster ad sales because *Hmong Today* can partner in approaching ad agencies and make the argument together that their media are worth supporting with ad dollars. In 2019, the monthly publication was still going strong and had an approximate audience of 25,000 readers.

In Wisconsin, there have also been two Hmong newspapers—*Wisconsin Hmong Life* was published in 1997–1998, and *Hmong Globe* started production in 2014 and is still printing in 2019. *Hmong Globe* is a quarterly newspaper printed by publisher Snyu W. Yang in both English and Hmong language, which is extremely rare in the Hmong American newspaper landscape. There have also been a number of Hmong magazines and online news sites that published one or two issues before ceasing to be updated (Leepreecha 2008). All the Hmong American newspapers described here are published primarily in English, with only occasional articles appearing in Hmong language. This may seem odd, given how many first-generation Hmong Americans primarily speak Hmong (along with some Lao or Thai language) and do not speak any English. Yet many of these elders do not have a high degree of literacy in Hmong or any other language. They are refugees of a war that disrupted their opportunities for schooling in Laos or Thailand, and arrived in the United States as adults and did not become formally educated. Hmong also developed their written language relatively recently, with missionaries to Laos establishing what is known as the Hmong Romanized Popular Alphabet (RPA) in the 1950s. Previous to this, Hmong culture was primarily oral, and there is a strong persistence of oral traditions that I discuss more in later chapters. For these reasons, Hmong newspapers and other printed materials largely target 1.5- or second-generation Hmong Americans (those who were born abroad but immigrated as a child, and those who were born in the United States, respectively) who are comfortable reading and writing in English.

Why View Micro Media Owners as Entrepreneurs?

I begin this analysis of Hmong newspaper industries by arguing that we must understand these micro media outlets and their founders in terms of entrepreneurship. In efforts to produce a meaningful source of news and information for their specific ethnic community, individuals who are already juggling full-time jobs and other duties additionally take on the enormous responsibility of running a newspaper for the Hmong community. All individuals who run media outlets are small business owners and managers, assuming financial risk and responsibility for the venture while managing its daily operations. But the term "entrepreneur" is reserved for business owners who create new businesses and do so in innovative or creative ways, challenging traditional modes of doing business (Achtenhagen 2008; Carland et al. 1984). The Hmong micro media industries analyzed here are constantly forced to innovate whenever they take an organizational structure that is usually populated with dozens or hundreds of workers and find ways to take on the same professional tasks with only a fraction of the personnel. With their low overhead costs and limited oversight, they can shift quickly and potentially find new opportunities for entrepreneurial innovation. As we will see, these innovations take many forms—including new ways of procuring financial investments and sales, reaching and engaging with audiences, and utilizing multimedia technologies.

The notion that Hmong newspaper owners are entrepreneurs is also reinforced through the notion of ethnic entrepreneurship, which is the practice of owning and operating a business that primarily engages with one's ethnic community (Volery 2007). Ethnic entrepreneurship is often synonymous with immigrant entrepreneurship, as both terms recognize that there are specific economic conditions facing recent immigrants and ethnic minorities that necessitate and lead to this form of self-employment. Zhou and Cho (2010) point out that scholarly investigations of ethnic entrepreneurship have often been limited to considerations of economic impact, and call for more consideration of noneconomic impacts. This study of media entrepreneurship certainly demands investigation beyond its economic impact, given the distinctive ways in which we understand the business of media. As Küng (2007) states, "Media firms are not thoroughbred commercial entities, but must also comply with public interest and artistic and creative imperatives" (24). Moreover, the mandate and mission of ethnic media are also frequently connected to public service values, such as providing information to an underrepresented community, helping to increase education about current affairs, or contributing to a stronger public sphere for ethnic minorities. We cannot fully align their interests with corporate media and market success, as there are clearly civic and community interests that also impact decisions.

If entrepreneurship is centered around discovery and exploiting business opportunities, the ethnic entrepreneur capitalizes on the fact that ethnic communities who are systematically marginalized are often eager to support a business that recognizes their specific needs and circumstances. Hmong American newspaper publishers frame their impetus for creating a news outlet in just this way, explaining that they were frustrated with mainstream coverage of their community and wanted to make a change. Steve Thao from the *Hmong Tribune* describes his goal as follows: "My goal was just to find positive news. Living in Fresno right after college, there was a wave of negative news about Hmong gangsters. I really wanted to find positive news about the community to change the narrative about our community, so I that's why I started the *Hmong Tribune*." Wameng Moua of *Hmong Today* also seeks to improve coverage of Hmong communities within a broader media landscape that excludes their perspective: "I can't consider myself standard media or standard journalism, I do advocacy journalism. Ethnic media is still viable and necessary because every single other media is narrated by the white voice. Ethnic media is the only one not run by the white viewpoint, it's the Hmong viewpoint for the Hmong community. That's why it's important to do what I do." These comments help to explain the political motivations for creating Hmong American newspapers that challenge mainstream media narratives and advocate for their own communities in entrepreneurial ways. Yet their newspapers are still businesses that need to be financially solvent, and there are many ways in which entrepreneurialism itself helps these publications innovate beyond the traditional business models for newspapers.

The traditional way that newspapers have been financially profitable is to sell reader subscriptions and sell advertisers the space for promoting their product to consumers. These are related to one another, as advertisers will pay more to reach larger numbers of readers and may not be interested in advertising at all to tiny niche audiences. For this reason, many small publications such as ethnic media opt to distribute their publications for free in order to boost their circulation numbers—reporting the number of copies distributed at newsstands, rather than simply the number of paid subscribers. Hmong American newspapers largely follow this trend. Their pages are filled with advertisements for Hmong restaurants, shops, real estate agents, insurance agencies, chiropractors, and service providers. To attract these advertisers, they work to frame their publication as the primary way to reach the Hmong American market and its specific commodity audience (Gentles-Peart 2014). Then they distribute their publications locally to Hmong markets and newsstands.

But beyond this particular revenue model, many Hmong micro media owners demonstrate their entrepreneurialism by developing and operating multiple interconnected media outlets. In many ways, the study of Hmong American newspapers demands expanding beyond this single medium to consider the relationship between newspapers and other media outlets and formats. This is certainly the case for Wameng Moua, the publisher of *Hmong Today*. After a decade of regularly hitting the pavement to find new advertisers for the paper, Moua felt like he had reached his limit. There just were not enough untapped corporations and individuals who were interested in reaching the Hmong American market, which meant his revenue streams could no longer increase. But his own skills as a photographer had developed considerably during the years he had taken photos for the newspaper, and people were asking if they could hire him as a photographer or documentary filmmaker. He decided to expand beyond running the newspaper to create a commercial photography and videography business called Zoom Creatives. In addition to the community prominence that Moua already gained from running the newspaper, this photography business also could benefit from registering as a Minority-Owned Business Enterprise. In Minnesota, there are a number of government certifications for small businesses owned by minorities and other economically disadvantaged groups (Mackay and Smith 2006). This certification then raises the profile of the small business by helping them to secure contracts with the state. Moua's photography service was then better positioned to financially support the newspaper.

In addition to operating the *Hmong Today* newspaper and photography business, Moua also participated in one more media outlet—he hosted a Hmong

American radio program at the community radio station KFAI 90.3 FM in Minneapolis for 11 years. The *HmongFM* program went on the air in 2006 with Moua and his sister Kathy Mouacheupao as cohosts. They played contemporary Hmong music and participated in conversations with a diverse variety of guests, including community organizers, politicians, and artists. They also had a news segment where they discussed recent stories that had been published in *Hmong Today*. Although I analyze the political and feminist content of *HmongFM* further in chapter 5, this of discussion of Moua's leadership in the Hmong newspaper, photography, and radio industries helps us to better understand how micro media industries can survive—by situating their products within a larger media empire that includes operating multiple businesses at once. To fully comprehend the way that entrepreneurism and the development of media empires shape and sustain Hmong American newspapers, we can also examine the place of Steve Thao's publication within the larger Hmong ecology.

Building a Hmong American Media Empire

Long before Steve Thao founded the *Hmong Tribune* in 1998, he had already been deeply involved with Hmong media through a family connection—his father Su Thao was a well-known Hmong movie mogul. Su Thao founded a video production company called ST Universal Video in 1990. At the time, consumer cameras for producing VHS content had just become affordable, and Su Thao had studied filmmaking at community college. One of ST Universal Video's primary products was videos from Thailand, India, and China that had been dubbed into Hmong language. But as one of the first Hmong Americans to return to Laos and Thailand, Su Thao also used his video camera and storytelling skills to capture documentary footage and narratives from the homeland. These videos included recordings from festivals and beauty pageants, often with voice-over narration, as well as music videos and dramatizations of folktales, war histories, and romantic stories. Louisa Schein (2002) argues that through these videos "Hmong could be seen to be making space for their very particularized narratives, ones that enunciate their own cultural memories, war genealogies, sentiments of loss, and struggles of resettlement" (241). Across Schein's body of scholarship on Hmong videos, we can see that video had become the predominant form of Hmong media in the 1990s and had a deep impact on Hmong American culture.

Steve Thao always had a vision for connecting Hmong Americans through media, and helping his father Su Thao run his video production business was just the beginning of his long career in developing media enterprises. In the late 1990s, their family ventured into the radio industry with ST Radio. They began by purchasing three hours a night for $300 at a Christian radio station in Fresno. If they sold advertisements to play during their time block, they could still turn

a profit. Steve Thao had moved to the Twin Cities and looked into radio programs there, but he struggled to find stations that would broker hours to the
Hmong community. He decided to partner with a friend and purchase a subchannel of an FM station in the Twin Cities. FM subchannels offer a cheaper
alternative to owning an entire radio station while also allowing full control
of programming (discussed further in chapter 4); the only catch was that listeners could only tune in through purchasing special radios. He eventually sold the
station to Peter Xiong and turned his attentions to the digital arena.

In 1997—a year before he started publishing his newspaper, the *Hmong
Tribune*—Steve Thao partnered with his niece Song Vang to create a web platform called Hmong Online. Vang had been a web designer and developer since
the mid-1990s and saw the rise of the world wide web as an important space
for growing a Hmong social network. She designed Hmong Online to allow
users to create their own profiles and then participate in messages boards, post
classified ads in a marketplace, chat with other users, find friends and romantic partners, and learn about events. The site also prominently advertised ST
Radio and ST Universal Video, including listing their entire video catalog and
facilitating video orders. At its peak, the site had around 30,000 active users
and attracted 200–300 people every day. Thao and Vang ran the site together
for nearly a decade, but eventually the cost of hosting the site was far greater
than their occasional advertising revenue and they shut it down.

Despite occasional losses and setbacks, the development of this interconnected media empire is clearly based around efforts to support the success of
each individual outlet. We can see the impact of this kind of synergy and innovation in the novel way the *Hmong Tribune* newspaper was distributed. The
newspaper was based out of the Twin Cities and had a limited number of
subscriptions—around one hundred, which would be mailed out individually.
The rest of the 20,000 newspapers printed every month then needed to be delivered to Hmong stores and other physical locations with news racks. For these
papers, Thao was able to piggyback on the distribution system that was already
in place for ST Universal Videos, which had a well-developed distribution network in place. Every month, they were sending their videos out to 300–400
Hmong grocery stores and markets across the country—including Minnesota,
Wisconsin, California, North Carolina, and other locations with Hmong communities. Along with the videos, they could include a packet of newspapers.
Their deployment of vertical integration meant that they could use the newspaper to promote their videos through reviews and other promotional pieces,
while the videos could include commercials for their other media ventures—
much like they had done with the Hmong Online website. Steve Thao admits
that he disliked the process of acquiring advertisers to support his newspaper,
so it was helpful to use these other businesses as a promotional platform.

Another one of Steve Thao's media productions was the public television program *Kev Koom Siab* (Path to Unity), which he produced from 1999 to 2005. This public affairs program was originally created in 1991 by producer Foung Hawj, who later became a member of the Minnesota Senate. The program's thirty-minute segments were broadcast through Twin Cities Public Television, in addition to wider distribution through the Saint Paul Neighborhood Network, the Minneapolis Television Network, and the International Channel. It was widely celebrated as the first Hmong American public affairs programs. *Kev Koom Siab*'s hosts helped educate the Hmong community about news and current events, with guest speakers who would discuss topics such as health, politics, education, and youth culture. Steve Thao took the position of executive producer at *Kev Koom Siab* to develop his skills in television production because he wanted to one day run a 24/7 Hmong television station. Then in 2005 he got a job offer to head back to Fresno and help start up a full-time radio station, KQEQ 1210 AM. He realized that if he wanted to continue learning more about operating his own station one day, this would be good experience, so he took the job. He was frequently frustrated with the lack of professionalism in Hmong media. He said, "Unfortunately there are not many people with a journalism background, so the news is just hearsay. There's no system for verification, and there's some silly things they put out there. I really believed in the responsibility of the media."

Steve Thao eventually came back to Minnesota, where he became the executive director of the Center for Hmong Arts and Talent (CHAT) in 2017. CHAT is an organization that promotes a wide range of arts and culture for Hmong Americans in the Twin Cities, including theater, visual arts, fashion, and music. They particularly focus on engaging Hmong youth with arts education. As my interview with Steve Thao concluded, he was preparing to drive the CHAT van to the local high school to pick up youth for their arts program. But he still sees this as connected to his aspirations in media: "I still had a dream about television, so I applied for the CHAT job. I wanted to take some of my video background and my journalism background and have a real television station. We could actually have a program to talk about social issues and support nonprofits. I see that vision, that television could create and support the system." Television and other forms of media remain interconnected in his vision for how Hmong communities will connect and grow.

Through these narratives we can see the way that newspapers like the *Hmong Tribune* and *Hmong Times* fit into a larger Hmong media ecology where individuals are able to build capital through the concentration of media ownership. Their decisions about financing, distribution, marketing, and skill development help us understand some of the unique ways in which micro media newspapers can overcome the specific challenges and limitations that come with their small size. Moua is able to financially support his newspaper through strengthening the skills that allow him to develop an additional media enterprise, as well as to take advantage of state policies designed to support minority enterprise. Thao is able to extend his distribution across the country through piggybacking off of shipping channels already in place, and to cross-promote his various media enterprises across multiple platforms. This macro-level investigation helps to reveal the interconnected ways in which the Hmong media landscape has developed.

In infrastructural terms, this case helps to reveal some of the limits and opportunities facing micro media entrepreneurship in their dependence on material resources. Ownership of a radio subchannel in the 1990s required that listeners purchase a special radio receiver for the sole purpose of tuning into the single Hmong radio station. While this kind of purchase might be justified if there was a lively sector of competing stations for listeners to toggle between, it was a difficult marketplace for technological pioneers in the early days (for a deeper exploration of adaptations to emerging platforms for audio media, see chapter 4). But the concentration of media ownership meant that there was possibility for material advantages if infrastructures could be used in innovative ways, such as the decision to utilize video store delivery routes for newspaper distribution.

We can also consider the impact of micro media enterprise on the workers who shape them—including their individual skill development, professional identity formation, and construction of communities of practice. As discussed earlier with regard to the one-man-band journalist, one of the impacts of shrinking newsrooms is the rise of multiskilling. This is when workers are required to develop a diverse range of job skills, rather than honing in on just one role. Given the extremely limited staff size behind Hmong micro media industries, founding or acquiring multiple media enterprises can be understood as the process through which those skills are developed. For Steve Thao, this meant being mentored by his father to learn about the video industry, hosting a radio show so he could learn more about the radio industry, and founding a Hmong digital platform so he could learn about online tools. Together, each of these opportunities increased his ability to successfully nurture his own media enterprises in newspaper, video, radio, and digital media because he could evolve into a more competent journalist, radio host, website developer, and other roles. The same is true for Wameng Moua, who admitted that he developed his professional skills in journalism after he had already founded *Hmong Today*. He stated, "If I went to journalism school I'd probably have to be really really good to be a newsroom journalist. I wasn't the best at first, but you craft your skills and you can do your own thing. I probably would never have made it in the newsroom at the *Pioneer Press* or *Star Tribune*, just going into it like I did. But when you train yourself, you become good enough for yourself." This story reveals the significance of individual learning on the development of micro media outlets, as some ethnic entrepreneurs may not have the resources or educational background to take on professional roles outside of their enterprises. Yet over time they become skilled, competent, and prepared for expansion.

There are also consequences for the way that micro media entrepreneurs develop their professional identities, given that one person must manage both the economic side of the business and the production of content (and quite often much more than that). The identities embodied by the micro media entrepreneur include small business owner, but also an amalgam of various media and creative professions—journalist, reporter, photographer, editor, and others. These dynamics are sometimes communicated through the pages of the newspaper itself, such as in one issue of *Hmong Today* where there was a pull-out box with images and bios for their four core staff members—the editor in chief, associate editor, graphic designer, and artistic director. The editor in chief is described as wearing "multiple hats, including a hefty load of the journalistic work" and two of the other individuals are described as balancing full-time jobs outside of *Hmong Today* ("Meet the Team of *Hmong Today*," 2005). The tone of each description seems to indicate that these four individuals are overburdened and heroic in their ability to juggle so many different responsibilities at the newspaper when it is merely a side gig. These hybrid identity formations can be complicated but have the potential to sustain participation in an extremely exhausting and all-encompassing line of work because they allow for a high degree of control in both the creative and financial arena. This kind of autonomy is important because the rise of deskilled labor can sometimes promote feelings of alienation and devaluation, where the media worker becomes a cog in a large machine and suffers from the loss of ownership and control (Hesmondhalgh 2010).

Hmong media entrepreneurs have the freedom to grow, develop skills, and engage in meaningful labor, but one aspect that may still be lacking within micro media industries is the constitution of a professional community. Charles Husband (2005) has argued that minority ethnic media personnel form "communities of practice," where "individuals work together by employing shared routines and complementary skills, and . . . new participants are socialised into the community" (463). For traditionally staffed ethnic media outlets, the newsroom can be seen as a significant community of practice because there is a sustained group of individuals coming together to learn, share knowledge, and develop a collective professional identity. Such communities of practice play an important role in developing professional competence and building job satisfaction. Matthew Matsaganis and Vikki Katz (2014) expand on Husband's research on ethnic media professionals by investigating the way that ethnic media producers can form identities through interactions with newsroom colleagues, but also with the ethnic communities that they serve. That is, in the absence of a robust newsroom or larger organizational structure, ethnic media producers may consider their audience to be part of their professional community.

The shifting of audience members from consumers to producers has become a common feature within many forms of ethnic media. While all media producers must consider the needs and desires of their audience in order to thrive, ethnic media face additional pressures. As Matsaganis and Katz argue, "Because ethnic media are often viewed as the community's voice, audience members can feel compelled to discipline producers they believe to be deviating from such roles" (937). The rise of participation from ethnic media audiences has also been seen in media across the globe. In his study of the rapid growth of ethnic media, Mark Deuze (2006) argues that the rise of participatory media cultures and audience-producers have played a significant role. Yet as mentioned earlier, Hmong forms of micro media are not necessarily premised on increasing participation, and their small size is often the result of a struggle to incorporate new voices. In the following analysis of Hmong newspapers and their audiences, we can see both forces at work—audience members clearly play an important role in providing feedback that strengthens the micro-staffed outlet, but this does not necessarily mean that the outlet embodies a participatory ethos or can easily transition audience members to staff members. These findings about audiences help to further differentiate micro media from our assumptions about both ethnic media and participatory media, despite some common features.

Engaging the Audience through Letters to the Editor

One of the main methods used to assess the relationship between media and its audience has been ethnography, with researchers interviewing audiences or observing interactions in person. This includes how media workers perceive their audiences, as well as how audiences respond to and engage with media texts. In the particular case of newspapers, the relationship between producers and readers is also made partially visible to the public through the letters to the editor section. The letters page opens up the opportunity for audience members to speak their mind and initiate a conversation with the newspaper, for the editors to put forward particular voices and negate others, and for the editors to directly respond to readers. It also can be understood as a limited public forum for discussing issues that are important to readers (Perrin 2016). Given the argument by Matsaganis and Katz that small ethnic papers view the readers they serve as an important component of their professional community, the letters page can help reveal some of the specific contours of that relationship. This next section is based on an analysis of the letters to the editor pages of both *Hmong Today* and the *Hmong Tribune,* so we can see if the small size of the newspaper shapes their relationship in meaningful ways. It shows the way that micro media entrepreneurs are unusually dependent on their audience to help support their outlets by shaping the discourse around professional media in their community, but that this openness to feedback is not necessarily premised on increasing participation in making media.

One of the most common types of letter printed in Hmong American newspapers is simply enthusiastic praise and gratitude. This includes letters expressing surprise at seeing a Hmong newspaper for the first time, eagerness to see the newspaper expand their distribution and coverage, and general responses such as being "impressed" and feeling "very uplifted" after reading it. Some letters articulate what they see as the goals of a Hmong newspaper, such as uniting Hmong people across the diaspora, promoting education about Hmong, or showing readers how successful Hmong Americans have been. There are also many letters expressing the hope that this newspaper will be more successful than other Hmong newspapers, such as this letter to the *Hmong Tribune*: "We subscribed to a few other newspapers in the past and they died down. Whatever you do, remember that we need this paper! . . . I am also delighted that you are giving us what a REAL newspaper should be giving us. A variety of articles touching on different topics" (November 1, 1998). This letter acknowledges the frequency of failure for other small newspapers in its plea for this paper to continue. But in its latter comments we also see an implicit critique of other Hmong media that are perceived to be less "REAL" due to their limited scope. This wish for media that discusses a diverse range of topics seems rather minimal, which further emphasizes the desire for merely increasing professionalism in the Hmong media landscape.

These messages of praise and support were the most frequent in the *Hmong Tribune*, which Steve Thao founded with the explicit goal of increasing positive coverage of Hmong Americans. Given this orientation, it makes sense that audience members would be pleased with stories that cast themselves and their community in a favorable light. These complimentary messages serve two functions—the writer is able to communicate to the editor which aspects are most appreciated and shape the direction of the publication, and the editor is able to promote the newspaper by facilitating the spread of positive responses and helping other readers understand how they could be appreciative as well. While a publication of any size might want to share glowing messages of support with their readers, these letters can be particularly helpful for a small publication that is largely supported by volunteer labor and could be terminated at any point by the editor simply deciding to move on to a different project.

But there are also many letters that are critical of the newspapers. The printing of these letters affirms the fact that ethnic media professionals are disciplined by their audience, but also helps us to understand that "positive coverage" is not the only demand by readers. In fact, many readers of the *Hmong Tribune* specifically request more controversial stories: "I would like to hear more controversial issues. I challenge you to be more on the edge and ask the tough questions. . . . We all talk among our small circle of friends for a better society and culture. We all talk about the ills of our people and the possible remedies. But no one does anything but talk among our safe little circle! I challenge you to put those questions in the public consciousness" (September 4, 1998). This letter contextualizes the communicative frameworks of some Hmong communities, where there is a desire for meaningful conversation to move beyond the private sphere and into the public sphere. This desire is also visible in the pages of *Hmong Today*, as editor Wameng Moua has a goal of openly attempting to address conflict within the community. As Moua stated to me in an interview: "We're not afraid to bring out our dirty laundry. We get criticized for it, but I tell them this is happening in our community, it's a toxic thing that needs to be spoken about and people need to learn about different perspectives. We're not afraid to say that's wrong." At one point, some of his readers staged a propaganda campaign with posters stating that he was a liar. It is for reasons like these that Moua does not publish under his real name and does not want anyone to know where he lives. One of the issues *Hmong Today* has frequently addressed is the problem of abusive international marriage in the Hmong community, where married Hmong men travel to Laos and court underage girls. Moua's paper also was not afraid to discuss an incident where General Vang Pao, a highly lauded Hmong community leader, had a foundation that was involved in questionable spending and improper financial solicitations.

Yet this does not necessarily mean that micro-sized outlets are responsive to the demands and complaints of their audience. Along with his desire to challenge the Hmong community through content, Moua has also used the flexibility of his small staff size to experiment with elements such as design. In December 2004, he drew an impassioned response from readers with a front-page story about a hunting tragedy where a Hmong American hunter named Chai Vang murdered six white hunters. To accompany the story about how Vang and other Hmong hunters often faced racism and physical violence while they were hunting, Moua used Photoshop to create a bumper sticker on the back of a pickup truck that read "Save a deer / Kill a Hmong." Although the image is labeled "a dramatization," many had reported seeing this actual bumper sticker on cars in the area (Whitehurst 2015, 171). Moua reported that readers did not approve of his use of Photoshop for the cover image and communicated their criticisms to him. The repercussions from this decision continued long afterward, even in discussions of topics that had no explicit connection to the Photoshopped image. For instance, two months later in response to an article about a Hmong couple that survived a tsunami, one letter said: "I am growing more and more skeptical about Wameng Moua and his stories or dramatizations. I believe there was no such Hmong couple. . . . Please prove that your source is credible" (January 27, 2005). Moua responded with a note from the editor that defended his decision. The use of the term "dramatization" in the reader's letter, which echoes the description of Moua's edited image from the previous issue, draws a connection between the decision to fictionalize the image and the resulting loss of credibility. The phrase "Wameng and his stories" also relies on direct address to name and belittle the newspaper as nothing more than one individual and his potentially fabricated stories, revealing some of the risks to reputation that are inherent to micro media outlets. It was common for many letter writers to address the publisher by first name in their salutation, rather than the more traditional "Dear Editor" or "To Whom It May Concern." The phrasing of "Dear Steve" or "Dear Cheu" indicates the fact that readers understood publications to be strongly associated with one individual, rather than a collective body or larger news organization. These understandings are then reinforced by the fact that the newspaper's writers, photo editors, or designers in question can defend their decisions and stand firm on them because the ultimate authority of the newspaper's editor or publisher is often the exact same individual.

These exchanges between newspaper readers and the editor-publishers who control content helps to show some of the ways in which Hmong audiences come to play an active role in articulating, debating, and shaping the professional codes and norms of the newspaper. As Matsaganis and Katz theorized, the audience can be viewed as an important component of the newspaper's professional community of practice—helping to bolster the features that are most successful, add coverage of topics and perspectives that are missing, and hold the paper accountable to professional ethics. In the absence of an extensive staff of professionals among whom these debates might play out behind the scenes, the editors of the paper construct relationships with their community of readers as a public way of performing these conversations.

Yet we can also consider the question of what we learn about a newspaper's openness to participation from the letters section. In some cases, the public airing of debates about professional norms can serve to bolster the authority of the publisher himself, rather than demonstrating an openness to considering the perspective of readers. Moreover, in some cases the newspapers have moved from an earlier phase of soliciting writing contributions and new staff members to eventually becoming more skeptical and pessimistic about onboarding new writers. Wameng Moua explained that he had often attempted to increase the size of his *Hmong Today* staff, but either could not afford to do so or did not have the resources to retain employees. He said: "I've tried hiring people, but if they're any good, once they get a job they're done. All the training I've done with you, you made a name for yourself and published stuff, and now you have a job somewhere else. That's happened three or four times." Although he likes the idea of newspapers providing an opportunity for education and professional development, his own investment had routinely come at a high personal cost. As a result, he eventually settled on an extremely small staff where he continues to do the bulk of the labor.

There are many forms of small-scale journalism that are premised on increasing participation and access—specifically, media outlets that identify within the tradition of "community media" focus on lowering barriers to entry and providing educational opportunities so everyday citizens can become media producers. Yet the Hmong micro media outlets described here are not necessarily premised on these participatory civic values. The editors of both *Hmong Today* and the *Hmong Tribune* clearly value input from their readers and seek to actively engage their perspectives. They spoke about how important it was to meet reader demands and interests, and they strove to make themselves available to community members. Nonetheless, for such small publications it can be prohibitively difficult to actually maintain openness to reader contributions and participation, and doing so may conflict with other values and goals.

Conclusion: Participation in Micro Media Newspapers

These questions about openness to participation and new voices are important to consider given that we can now see how Hmong newspapers are indeed part of the larger trend of media conglomeration. While Hmong media outlets have not been acquired by mainstream media corporations, it is still the case that media power within the Hmong community is concentrated in the hands of an extremely small number of individuals. At a global level, there has always been great skepticism and concern about the power of media moguls like Rupert Murdoch, Michael Bloomberg, and Jeff Bezos who acquire media enterprises across different sectors (news, film, digital media, music, book publishing, etc.) in ways that are feared to threaten our democracy (Baker 2006). In the case of concentrating media ownership within ethnic media industries and micro media industries, we can still consider the question of how such publications contribute to or undermine democratic participation. Opposition to media concentration has long posited that "the basic standard for democracy . . . [is] a very wide and fair dispersal of power and ubiquitous opportunities to present preferences, views, vision. This is a democratic distribution principle for communicative power" (Baker 2006, 7). Community media have long served as a counterpoint to media concentration in attempting to preserve democratic ideals, but these Hmong newspapers do not share a participatory ethos.

The fact that Hmong newspapers are becoming less participatory contrasts with other understandings of how contemporary ethnic media are developing. While audience feedback is important, we see very little blurring of boundaries between consumer and producer. In Deuze's (2006) study of ethnic media as participatory media he specifically accounts for the existence of this possibility, as the concept of convergence culture casts a wide enough net to include both citizens' media and commercial media. Here we see an example of small ethnic media outlets that retain a commercial sensibility and hierarchical relationship to audience members, even amid their efforts to support their communities. These findings can help us to reexamine other categories of small journalism such as rural journalism outlets serving sparsely populated geographic regions and digital journalism such as blogs that we might otherwise assume fit into the politicized category of "citizens' media." Further, the micro media industry examined here helps us to keep an eye out for the way these shifts in media production contribute in some cases to a micro media empire—where one individual owns and operates a wide variety of media outlets that can develop from one another. These Hmong media conglomerates constitute important networks even in the absence of the digital media that are often assumed to form the basis for contemporary communication networks. Together they help us to understand some of the unique aspects of micro media newspaper outlets, their relationship to micro media industries, and the innovative ways that ethnic media are developing in spite of their limits.

3

TV without Television

• •

YouTube and Digital Video

Mee spends most of her days at home watching over her two young grandchildren, which she admits can get a little monotonous. It was wintertime when the forty-seven-year-old and her family first moved to Madison, Wisconsin, from a refugee camp in Thailand, and she felt even more isolated from her relatives and friends. But that was five years ago, and now her college-aged daughter bought her an iPad Mini and taught her how to use Facebook and YouTube on it. She explained how much this has changed her life: "I'm so grateful that here in America we can connect through the multimedia. That helps me to manage my emotions a little bit more and the day doesn't seem as long as it was before. Because I can watch songs and listen to the news and that helps a lot." I ask her to show me how she uses the iPad, and she swipes her finger across the device to open the YouTube app. Although she has limited literacy, family members had taught her the Romanized alphabet and she carefully starts to type out the letters "H-M-O." At this point, a number of options begin to autocomplete and she clicks on the term "Hmong." She is then able to scroll through a bottomless feed of videos focusing on Hmong topics, nearly all of which are Hmong news reports. She sees an image of a news program that looks appealing, so she clicks to watch it and the accompanying videos that are similar to it.

This story reflects an extremely common way for Hmong Americans to engage with Hmong media in a way that is completely distinct from the print newspapers discussed in the previous chapter. Hmong audiences with low levels of literacy have little use for newspapers, but digital technologies and platforms have opened up a wealth of new opportunities for consuming and engaging with news media and other forms of audiovisual information. When Mee searched for the term "Hmong," she was greeted with YouTube videos from Hmong American outlets like Suab Hmong News, Hmong TV Network, 3HMONGTV, and Hmong TV 24 Hours. These outlets provide weekly content that includes reporters reading news reports from behind desks, field reports covering Hmong events on location, interviews with Hmong leaders and professionals, and clips from community events such as pageants and festivals. While the news content in these videos may be similar to the kinds of stories covered in Hmong American newspapers, the transformation of news from print to audiovisual digital outlets demands close examination for a number of reasons.

We can begin by considering the production cultures and industrial context for these Hmong digital news outlets, all of which fall under the category of micro media outlets due to their small staff size. If the previous chapter's examination of micro-staffed newspaper outlets revealed how entrepreneurialism and innovation are the basis for survival amid resource limitation, what are the specific challenges faced by video and digital outlets such as these, and how do they address these challenges? In closely examining four forms of Hmong television (Hmong TV Network, 3HMONGTV, Hmong TV 24 Hours, and Suab Hmong News), we can see how an extremely small staff is able to produce audiovisual content that is recognized as "television." Yet it also can be seen as an example of a hybrid media platform, as these news outlets challenge some of the core concepts we use to understand the medium of television in the digital era.

This chapter addresses the digital textuality of these programs and the impact of digital affordances on micro media users. As we can see from the way that Mee seeks out content on YouTube, the technological affordances of the platform deeply shape the experience of users and audiences in engaging with Hmong online news. This includes how the search function operates, what options are revealed through auto-complete, which videos are included as a result of her search, how the content of the video is advertised, and what happens after a video is selected and viewed. These factors have different meanings for users with differing levels of both digital literacy and reading/writing literacy, and shape the way that content travels through the larger Hmong network of users. Since Hmong micro media entrepreneurs often do not have the resources or technological expertise to create or operate their own platforms, they rely on the platforms and digital infrastructures that are available to them—in this case, their use of YouTube means that they must fall prey to the ways its algorithms and interfaces shape engagement and possibility for their audiences.

To better understand how this form of television is understood by actual audience members, I examine a controversial moment that occurred with the outlet Hmong TV 24 Hours. When the channel's owner posted a video that rankled viewers due to its misogynistic content, they responded with an outpouring of conversation about the outlet itself. These comments help us to understand the power dynamics of the broader Hmong television landscape and the specific place of Hmong micro media outlets within it. In particular, it demonstrates the fact that it is possible for micro media industries and hybrid media platforms to effectively conceal the realities of their small size—an outcome that is shored up through the ways that they imitate the norms of mainstream media and gain power and legitimacy in doing so. This legitimacy, coupled with the fact that all decisions about any micro media outlet rest in the hands of limited individuals, can make micro media outlets surprisingly similar to mainstream media industries in being resistant to change and impervious to outside pressures.

Hmong Television as Micro Media Industry

The Hmong video news landscape is organized in ways that parallel the Hmong newspaper industry. It is dominated by a small group of Hmong American men, including Ying Fang and Koua Lee of Hmong TV Network, Mitch Lee of 3HMONGTV, Doua Chialy Her of Hmong TV 24 Hours, and Richard Wanglue Vang of Suab Hmong News. Though they each have worked alone, their stories converge along similar axes. They wanted to improve the lives of Hmong Americans by giving them access to information and educational materials that would help them connect to Hmong across the diaspora. Facing limited opportunities for building audiences and enticing advertisers who could financially support a television station, they turned to the digital realm. Armed with a camera and video-editing software, they began to create a wealth of televisual content and broadcast it to Hmong audiences. Despite the fact that they all strive to create television, their hybrid media platforms actually challenge many of the conventions of television and show how micro media industries innovate on traditional media formats as they navigate the limitations of small size.

Of these four Hmong television outlets, Hmong TV Network most fits the traditional definition of television. Since 2009, they have broadcast from a digital low-power television station with the call letters KJEO (channel 32.6) out of Fresno, California, and KJNK (channel 25.3) out of St. Paul, Minnesota. This means that residents in these geographic areas can use an antenna to access the channel for free on their television set. The channel actually originated as an all-digital streaming service in 2008, using a format called Internet Protocol television. Audiences could purchase a subscription to their service and watch content online (at hmongtvnetwork.com) or through a television set-top unit.

This mode of distribution was low cost for Hmong TV Network, but it was difficult to bring in advertisers. Hmong companies that might be interested in purchasing ads were largely local to cities with large Hmong American populations, which meant that they were less interested in targeting a geographically dispersed national or global audience. In 2009, a local digital television channel became available for leasing in Fresno, and Hmong TV Network jumped on the opportunity. With their move to local broadcast, the station became more appealing to advertisers—even as the costs for maintaining the station increased. In 2015, they added a channel in St. Paul as well.

Hmong TV Network has a small staff size, consistent with other micro media industries, making it remarkable that it is distributed via traditional terrestrial television broadcast. Like most Hmong media outlets, it is family owned and operated—the executive team includes owner and CEO Koua Lee, his daughter Thoua Lee, who is treasurer and secretary, her husband Ying Fang, who is president, and two other partners. Beyond this staff of five are the news anchors and show hosts, all of whom are volunteer staff who contribute their talent and time. Together they produce a number of regular shows, the most consistent of which is their news programming that airs Monday through Friday at 8 A.M. Their news anchors cover a wide range of topics ranging from local and U.S. news to global news that impacts Hmong in countries like Laos, Thailand, China, and France. Hmong TV Network also produces a number of talk shows focusing on topics like health, education, and youth issues. In between these shows, they broadcast Hmong movies and documentaries, and recordings from live performances of singing, pageants, and speeches.

This balance of offering very few original programs and filling the rest of the hours of the day with recycled content is on par with much of American television programming. Since the origination of commercial television in the 1940s, old films and repeats of programs have dominated the airwaves and left little time for live performances. Rather than understanding television as a conduit for live broadcasts, television has always been "a machine of repetition, geared toward the constant recirculation of recorded, already-seen events" (Kompare 2004, xi). While the economics of television programming have shifted over the years in response to audience needs and technological developments, it has always been cheaper to purchase television shows and films in syndication than to create a constant flow of new programming. Hmong television stations benefit even more from the economics of repetition because the informal economy within which Hmong media are created and shared means it is rare for payments to be exchanged in order to acquire broadcasting rights for Hmong content.

For Hmong audiences living in the diaspora with no homeland of their own, this array of television programming is deeply meaningful. Repeated viewings of familiar movies and performances provide connection and nostalgic longing, while informative current affairs programming helps educate viewers about political dynamics and cultural debates. Yet one kind of programming that is beyond the reach of this micro media industry is scripted television—including sitcoms, soap operas, cartoons, science fiction, fantasies, procedurals, and all other forms of serial and episodic storytelling. This absence is particularly noteworthy given the disproportionate amount of cultural value that is placed on scripted programming. As Elana Levine (2008) argues, discourses around media have problematically shifted toward celebrating the cultural elevation of scripted television, while live programs such as news, sports, and talk remain denigrated as merely "TV." Indeed, in 2015 FX Networks executive John Landgraf coined the phrase "Peak TV" in an assessment of "the unprecedented amount of scripted programming being produced" (Landgraf 2018), using the term "TV" to exclusively refer to scripted original series. The medium of television is constantly shifting to accommodate cultural and technological changes, but there is a general sentiment that the most "important" kind of both television and TV consists of scripted programming. When stations like Hmong TV Network consistently operate with only the barest of staff members, they simply do not have the personnel or financial support for narrative storytelling.

This is not to say that narrative forms of media production are impossible with a limited staff size. Indeed, there are many successful YouTube web series that demonstrate the potential for creating televisual content within extreme resource limitations, as Aymar Jean Christian has investigated. Christian argues that we must rewrite our understanding of legacy television to make room for a new kind of "open TV" where "independent producers, entrepreneurs, and fans are creating their own media system" (Christian 2018, 5) by distributing their content online. From his research, he estimates that each individual series is produced with a budget in the thousands to tens of thousands and narrates a story about creative labor that mirrors many of the conventions of independent film production. This includes "writing a script with modest ambitions, soliciting favors, trading resources, or hiring crew with multiple skills" (60). Yet even with an enormous supply of creativity, ambition, and goodwill, the production of small independent television series is a demanding and all-encompassing endeavor for the individuals at the helm. Christian describes the labor of the independent television producer as including a multitude of tasks, including story conception, production management, marketing, and fundraising. In the case of micro media television outlets like Hmong TV Network where network executives are already responsible for overseeing commercial contracts, maintaining online streaming technologies, billing, online registration, and more, the labor of producing scripted television has been simply untenable.

Such an absence is not unique to Hmong television, as the role of local television stations in the United States has always been to simply produce local news and public affairs programming. This includes a wide variety of potential topics, including unscripted programs for children, religious programming, educational programs, and discussions of topics such as business, agriculture, computers, law, health, music, and sports (Bishop and Hakanen 2002). Scripted content is then delivered to local stations through the national television networks and through syndication—including first-run syndication series like *Baywatch* and *Xena: Warrior Princess* airing for the first time, and second-run syndication that includes reruns of popular programs like *Friends* and *Seinfeld*. This is not to say that the relationship between local television stations and scripted content is ideal or without concern. Jonathan Nichols-Pethick (2009) worries that "since local stations rely heavily on syndicated material to fill out their programming schedules and lead viewers into their local news, more ownership power in the hands of the large media conglomerates that produce much of this programming, such as Disney, NBC Universal, or News Corp., could create an unbalanced playing field for access to these valuable programs" (158). But it explains who is responsible for supplying the staggering quantities of scripted programming to television outlets across the United States and what kinds of resources are traditionally required for doing so.

There are many other ethnic media television stations across the United States that lack the capacity required for scripted programming. Most often, they are able to run scripted programs originating in their home countries (e.g., Korean dramas, Indian sitcoms, and Venezuelan telenovelas). As has already been stated, there is no such possibility for Hmong media, given that there is no Hmong television industry anywhere in the world. This means that the closest thing to Hmong scripted television is simply dubbed versions of programming from other countries, such as the increasingly popular Thai television dramas (Jirattikorn 2018) or the limited number of Lao programs. Since many Hmong Americans speak Lao or Thai in addition to Hmong, television programs in those languages can sometimes be enjoyed without translation. But the limited size of Hmong broadcast outlets in the United States does shape the kinds of content that exist within the category of Hmong television.

To continue this interrogation of Hmong television further, we can move beyond exploring the production of content to consider how this form of television is consumed. Indeed, the television set itself often played a central role in the Hmong homes I visited, as it does in many American homes (Spigel 1992). While I conducted interviews with Hmong families, we sat together in the living room, where couches and chairs were arranged to face the television. In many cases the television would be on even if no one seemed to be watching, or a family member would resume watching the television at some point while we were chatting. This was helpful for me to observe, as I could get a sense for the way that television provided a backdrop to daily life. One woman in her fifties explained that she could not speak or understand English, but still liked to have the television on all throughout the day. She said, "I can't watch anything Hmong through the TV, I just watch the weather channel to see what the weather is like. If we had the internet through our TV, I might do that. But I don't like to waste a lot of time on videos." She clearly appraised the relative value of different forms of media consumption and made the decision that ambient American television was the form that fit best with her lifestyle.

There was an extremely wide variety within the ways Hmong American families used their television set. Sometimes it was only used for watching American television, whether or not the audience had sufficient English fluency for the programs to make sense. Others never used the television to access American programming, preferring instead to use it to access different forms of Hmong content. This included using the television set to watch old VHS and DVD movies or home videos. Many living rooms were lined with stacks and stacks of DVD cases. These had been acquired from sellers at Hmong shopping centers like those in St. Paul, where amid the rows of small shops set up inside large warehouses were always a handful that focused solely on DVDs. Community events like Hmong New Year and soccer tournaments also often included pop-up shops selling CDs and DVDs.

For those who did watch Hmong television channels like Hmong TV Network, there were many different ways of accessing content—including purchasing a set-top box, adding the channel through an over-the-top streaming device called Roku, or casting it from a digital device like a laptop or iPad. One family I visited was very lively with four young boys who were eager to demonstrate all of the different ways they engaged with screens from their living room. The seven-year-old easily moved from playing video games on the family's shared desktop computer to casting YouTube videos from the computer to a flat-screen television mounted on the wall. This was one way that families could watch Hmong TV Network content together, as the outlet uploaded many programs to their YouTube channel to make it accessible from any internet-ready device. While we know that television sets can be used for purposes that would not be considered "television" (such as playing video games or video chatting), these ways of accessing Hmong TV Network also remind us that contemporary television extends to all screen technologies. Recall users like Mee, who was described earlier as someone who engages with video content only through her iPad. She can easily navigate to content produced by Hmong TV Network by searching for "Hmong TV" on YouTube.

Yet not all YouTube content can or should be considered television, given that there is such a wide range of video content available on the platform. This is a meaningful distinction to draw for Hmong news in particular, because when we look at the other forms of Hmong video news that are available on YouTube, we can see more clearly how Hmong TV Network is unique. While the video content they post online consists of rebroadcasts from programming that originally aired on terrestrial television, there are many forms of Hmong video news that are *exclusively* digital, available only through YouTube channels, websites, and mobile apps. In the next section, I examine the three most popular outlets that operate in this form—3HMONGTV, Hmong TV 24 Hours, and Suab Hmong News. These hybrid media platforms help to expand and redefine the category of micro media television, revealing the significance of digital affordances in shaping the possibilities for Hmong televisuality.

YouTube Television and All-Digital Television Outlets

We can see from the story of Hmong TV Network that the struggles to operate a traditionally advertiser-supported television outlet are nearly insurmountable. Indeed, Hmong TV Network originally tried to bypass these difficulties by utilizing Internet Protocol television technologies. Even though they succumbed to the economics of advertising by rooting their station in geographic communities with large Hmong populations, they still heavily promote the unbounded reach of their station as it is accessed through digital technologies. One of the solutions to this problem is to exist only online, which alleviates the need to appease local advertisers and expands the potential reach to global members of the diaspora. This is the decision that was taken up by 3HMONGTV, Hmong TV 24 Hours, and Suab Hmong News—three all-digital outlets that are modeled after television broadcasts, but are not actually broadcast on television. There are many mainstream journalists and media personalities who operate in this way and deploy the same digital distribution logics. For instance, the online news network The Young Turks is led by former MSNBC commentator Cenk Uygur, who has been called "the most widely watched political talk show host you've never heard of" (Zax 2014) because his content is only available online through YouTube, Hulu, and Current TV. Similarly, the Al Jazeera Media Network established an online-only news channel called AJ+ in 2012 that provides news coverage from around the world and is completely separate from Al Jazeera's cable and satellite channels. Yet examples such as these represent companies that are worth millions of dollars and employ dozens of staff members to collectively produce content and run every aspect of the outlet. Like all Hmong micro media outlets, Hmong digital television operates on an extremely limited budget and depends on a limited amount of volunteer support to provide news anchors and on-screen talent. If we look closer at what is produced by these three prominent Hmong online video networks and what is happening behind the scenes, we can see how closely they fit the model of micro media industry developed in the previous chapter.

First, the primary content produced by these three Hmong outlets is video news programming. The videos are professional in their aesthetics and well versed in the semiotics of news broadcasting. Viewers can instantly recognize the visual tropes of the classic news broadcast—including splashy digital title sequences set to theme music, network bugs watermarked at the bottom of the screen, and chyrons identifying the topic or speaker. News reports are read by a news anchor who wears a dark suit or Hmong formal costume and looks directly into camera from behind the desk. Edited packages shot from the field and clips from live events are interspersed between comments from the news anchor at the desk.

While each of these news programs look as though they were produced by a well-staffed professional news team, the reality is that there are only one or two individuals behind the scenes working on each video. For instance, in many videos produced by Suab Hmong News, Richard Wanglue Vang is credited as producer, news correspondent, news anchor, video editor, and postproduction. His wife Maylee Vang and his longtime assistant Victor Vaj also help with some aspects of Suab Hmong News, such as videography and field reporting, but Richard takes on the lion's share of the work. As he said to me in an interview, "I'm the owner, the executive producer, the anchor, reporter, all the graphics, the music, everything technically." I asked him to describe what it looks like when he covers a story and he described every decision, large and small, that rested on his shoulders: sorting through news tips and story leads to find which ones are most important, working with community leaders to build trust and confidence, contacting sources, making sure they are prepared for media coverage, traveling to events with equipment, operating the camera and facilitating interviews, editing footage, adding sound and digital effects, and uploading content to his digital outlets. He does have a limited crew of additional camera operators who are able to assist by shooting footage in the Twin Cities, California, and across Wisconsin, particularly when they are covering extensive events like Hmong New Year festivities. But Richard estimates he spends twenty-five hours a week on Suab Hmong News—which he considers "full time," even though he also has a full-time day job working as a software engineer in Milwaukee, Wisconsin.

Suab Hmong News began in 1999 as a brokered Hmong language radio program that broadcast five hours a week and could be accessed locally in Milwaukee. At the time there was very little Hmong media, and Richard Wanglue Vang wanted to create something that would help the Hmong community. Vang describes his decision to create a website for the radio program: "In the year 2000 technology wasn't like it is now, we just put a link on the website. But people started listening nationally and internationally, and the website started getting hit really heavily—like 40 to 50,000 hits per day from all over the world." As their audience grew, he decided local radio was no longer meeting his needs; he felt constrained by the need to meet Federal Communications Commission (FCC) guidelines as well as the hustle to acquire sponsors to off-set the cost of brokering the time. Suab Hmong Radio moved to an all-digital format with a digital radio platform called Block Talk Radio, and increased its programming to daily offerings.

In 2005, Richard's brother-in-law Atari Xiong started up an Asian cable tele-vision channel called Crossings TV out of central California that broadcasts Chinese, Vietnamese, Filipino, Hmong, South Asian, and Russian language programming. With his newfound success in television, Atari convinced Richard he should expand beyond radio and consider creating video content for Hmong audiences. Richard was already a photography hobbyist, and learning videog-raphy came naturally to him. He decided to change Suab Hmong News into an umbrella company called Suab Hmong Broadcasting, and created current affairs videos to air on both Crossings TV and his own YouTube channel. These kinds of videos are now the primary output of Suab Hmong Broadcast-ing, which also shares news articles alongside the videos on their website. Rich-ard rents a small studio for hosting interviews, but many news segments are shot at Richard's home studio where he can record directly on his computer to streamline editing.

While traditional television stations like Hmong TV Network rely on the classic monetization model of soliciting advertisers and running commercials, stations that broadcast on YouTube have far greater flexibility in their business structure. For instance, when Suab Hmong News terminated their broadcast radio station, they stopped soliciting advertising altogether. Their YouTube channel does generate a small amount of advertising revenue from the ads that are automatically administered on the platform by Google AdSense. Other-wise, the outlet is financially supported through Richard's personal contribu-tions, occasional donations from Hmong supporters, and paid videography gigs like recording Hmong New Year events. As Richard describes it: "What we do now is for the Hmong community, so we don't really do business. It doesn't matter, our goal is to have people watch. It's not a business where we focus on where we get more money. Our goal is to have more people exposed to our pro-grams." In this sense, Suab Hmong News embodies the community-oriented mission of community media, which generates only enough revenue to keep the lights on and pay for costs such as website hosting and equipment.

The video news company 3HMONGTV is similar in format and produc-tion style to Suab Hmong Broadcasting. It is owned by Mitch Lee, an experi-enced videographer who has a passion for Hmong television. The name 3HMONGTV plays off the word for "three" in Hmong, *peb*, which also is the collective pronoun "we." As with other micro media entrepreneurs, Lee has developed multiple skills over the years so that he can single-handedly produce his video news programs. He explains: "I do the editing and the cutting, the scheduling, I go out there and shoot. Sometimes I get tired of it, but basically that's what I do now. If a story breaks I go out and cover it. It's a one-man show." He relies heavily on volunteer labor, particularly for on-screen talent, as he is a rare Hmong TV entrepreneur who does not regularly appear as an anchor. Yet he also attributes some of his success to the strong commitment of his volunteers, who have been loyal to the outlet for many years. He described to me: "I think it's better than if you pay for them. If you pay somebody and you expect them to do certain things and you have to train them, then it defeats the purpose of paying them. Most of these people are people who want to do a good job but they haven't gone to school for broadcast or journalism so you really have to teach them to do it. Once they know how to do it, I found that's more effective because they want to be there and be part of it." This sentiment is similar to the attitude of newspaper owners as described in the previous chapter, who struggled because the investment of time that it demands to train their staff members can make them more likely to take up jobs elsewhere. As Lee describes, this training can become more of a long-term investment if there is no promise of financial reward, and instead a strong reliance on community-oriented values.

Like Suab Hmong News, one way that he is able to financially support the outlet is by offering a number of videography services for hire, including recording community events, concerts, graduations, oral storytelling, documentaries, and others. These services are highlighted on the 3HMONGTV website (hbctv.net) as one of the five options on the main menu. While Suab Hmong News does accept advertising and uses its website to solicit new advertisers, its core mission is still to provide a community service. Mitch Lee from 3HMONGTV describes the Hmong media landscape and his own personal goals for his company: "I always hope the Hmong community can have more TV stations, but we don't have the funding or the manpower to do it. For me, this really grew out of passion. I didn't do this for money. If I were to do this for money, I would find a second job. But I have a goal and I have a passion and I have a service to the Hmong community." We can see from this quote that Lee is one of the few micro media entrepreneurs for whom Hmong media is not a side job, it is his full-time commitment.

This pattern of entrepreneurship is similar for Hmong TV 24 Hours, a news station owned by Doua Chialy Her. Her has no other employees, though his daughter Nancy Her and a number of family members provide ad hoc volunteer labor with various aspects of running the station. After studying video production at a technical college in Minnesota, Her started his first media company in 1989—a movie production company called Hmong USA Video Production. His early films included a romance called *Kev Hlub Txiav Tsis Tau*, a story about bride kidnapping called *Zij Poj Niam*, and an action film about the history of Hmong military called *Toj Xeem Paj Caj in 1979*. He also dubbed films into Hmong language, with a library of over one hundred titles from China and Hong Kong. In 2003, Her closed his video production companies in order to found the umbrella Hmong Corporation that includes Hmong Business Directory, Radio Hmong, and Hmong TV. These different outlets have experimented with a number of different emerging sound broadcasting technologies over the years, including radio programs that were delivered through the phone lines and DSL/cable, satellite radio, and internet radio. The outlet called Hmong TV (or Hmong TV 24 Hours) is distributed only online, streaming at www.hmongtv.com and through videos posted to the Hmong-TV24Hrs YouTube channel.

This wide array of media outlets has necessitated a number of different business models for Doua Chialy Her's corporation. Products like DVDs or streaming movies make money from direct audience payments, while his television network is supported through selling ads and placing them on his website or interspersing commercials among videos. In addition, Her promotes a number of different direct sales opportunities and multilevel marketing products such as Seacret and LifeVantage, all of which are advertised throughout the Hmong TV 24 Hours YouTube channel. This includes stand-alone video commercials (as in a video titled "Hmong Tv Why You Join Webtalk Becouse [sic] I need FREE money -TAU NYIAJ DAWB"), advertorials that feature Her's own instruction and commentary (for instance, "HMONG TV: HOW TO USE SEACRET Product By Doua Chialy"), and the use of Her's commercials to lead into or break up news videos.

Digital Television: Liveness and Flow in the Era of the Algorithm

The digital interfaces provided by these online news programs can help us to better understand how Hmong television constitutes a micro media industry that relies on digital technologies. While the Suab Hmong News outlet is structured like a traditional online news portal that delivers articles and videos, both Hmong TV 24 Hours and 3HMONGTV clearly emphasize "television" in their names and deliberately frame their offerings as Hmong television. The 3HMONGTV webpage that provides information for potential advertisers makes this framing clear: "Television remains the #1 source for news and information. It offers your business the opportunity to be seen and heard by utilizing sight, sound, and motion. TV is still the most efficient and effective method to reach a mass audience." In conversations with owners Doua Chialy Her, Mitch Lee, and also Steve Thao (as mentioned in the previous chapter), it is clear that Hmong television remains the pinnacle aspiration for them as media entrepreneurs. While they may be differentiated from traditional television behind the scenes, they also strive to model their offerings like television in many ways.

One of the primary ways that Hmong TV 24 Hours and 3HMONGTV model their services after television is by offering a "livestream" on their own websites. In doing so, they reproduce one of the defining characteristics of the television medium—televisual flow. Raymond Williams (1974) argued that the planned flow of television programs that are interspersed with advertisements and other promotional materials helps us to contextualize content within the broader televisual landscape. The livestream of Hmong television available at http://hbctv.net/live or https://www.hmongtv.com offers a programmed sequence of commercials and promotional content along with their own television programs, which include news broadcasts, talk shows and interviews, religious programming, and documentary footage of cultural events such as pageants and musical performances. In a conversation with Doua Chialy Her and his daughter Nancy about the programming, they described their programming decisions.

NANCY: He's always wanted to do the Hmong TV thing. That started off with the livestreaming online. It's not on TV. Nobody watches TV anymore, everyone does Netflix, Hulu, YouTube. No one sits there and watches TV, no one has the time to sit there, everyone's so busy now. The livestream is for the older generation who are just sitting at home.

DOUA: We make a loop of old programs and play them. I watch internet cable TV like CNN and NBC and they play loops too. No one can be there live 24/7. I copy them.

We can see two motivating factors for their formatting—the movement of audiences from broadcast television to digital outlets, and the sense that professional television stations also rely on repetition to fill the endless hours of airtime.

The delivery of televisual flow by these two outlets is also consistently framed as "live," as we can see through the use of the terms "livestream" and "live" used to label this content. The quality of liveness has historically been attached to television in ways that are similar to common uses for radio and mobile phone communication. For television, this term described the fact that broadcasts can automatically transmit footage from events as they are occurring, with little editing or manipulation. But as mentioned earlier, the programming schedule for television stations has always relied heavily on prerecorded footage, edited shows, and repeats or rebroadcasts of old programming. Yet even when the programming is not actually being broadcast live, there is another sense of liveness that comes from the fact that the television viewing public shares in the unfolding of content at the same time, in the same sequence. For the "older generation who are just sitting at home," as Nancy describes, the livestream of Hmong digital television produces a flow of content that is experienced simultaneously with other viewers across the diaspora.

This kind of engagement with audiences is part of what makes Hmong television a valuable and desirable format for Hmong media entrepreneurs. Mitch Lee describes the way that he wishes his YouTube channel was more like television, which he described as having audiences who know to tune in at a regular time of day for reliable updated content. He has worked toward this kind of consistency by creating a number of distinct programs, each helmed by a news personality—for instance, *Xav Paub Xav Pom* with Padee Yang, *Hmong American Weekly* with Chonburi Lee, the *Yia Michael Thao Show*, and a number of others. But Lee still feels like the station has not established enough consistency and regularity for audiences to know exactly when they can expect each show to air. He says, "We know that we have a need for those things in our community and we haven't really gotten a real show going. We want to put a new show out there and keep it going. We don't want to have it just show up every once in a while, we want to come in on a weekly basis and have a host who manages the show and does the show." Lee is humble in explaining his struggles to develop the kind of dependable programming his audiences demand, as his station does have many shows that produce consistent content. But in this explanation we can see that the small size of the staff plays a role in limiting his ability to produce content as quickly and reliably as he would like. Lee is currently responsible for nearly every aspect of producing each program, with the hosts simply showing up to provide the on-screen talent. He envisions a more sustainable future model in which each program's hosts also play a substantial role in producing, shooting, and editing their shows. This would demand intensive training in media production in the beginning, but would relieve some of the labor demands from falling only to Lee.

Lee's sense that he has not yet reached his goals as a television station are also limited by confining his notion of success to the way that audiences engage with broadcast television. If we expand beyond the notion of "providing content on a reliable hourly schedule," we can more clearly understand how successful the 3HMONGTV YouTube channel has been. Indeed, the YouTube channel is a thriving outlet for new content with a deep catalog of programming that users can selectively consume and engage with. In September 2018, the 3HMONGTV YouTube channel had over 24,000 subscribers and contained over 1,400 videos posted since 2010. This extremely large database of content is organized into more accessible YouTube playlists by show; *Xav Paub Xav Pom* has 148 videos, *Hmong American Weekly* has 19 videos, and the *Yia Michael Thao Show* has 27 videos. The same is true for the Hmong TV 24 Hours YouTube channel, which had over 40,000 subscribers and over 2,500 videos posted since 2013.

But there are also many ways in which a reliance on YouTube as a platform for distributing these video programs requires submitting to its specific affordances and possibilities. Indeed, with the profound influence of YouTube (as a company owned by Google) as the go-to platform for digital video distribution, its usage must be considered infrastructural in our need to question its impact on marginalized users and audiences (Plantin and Punathambekar 2019). For many of the Hmong users I talked to, YouTube was not simply one of many apps or websites used for finding videos—the YouTube app represented the entire category of video itself, as it was the only mechanism they knew how to use for accessing digital videos. If this is the case, then we must closely consider the impact of its interface, such as the fact that YouTube channels disrupt the concept of a preprogrammed flow by offering a catalog of previously recorded videos that can be accessed in any order. Together they comprise a digital archive that allows users to easily locate past programs that are hosted indefinitely for free. All digital content is paradoxically stable and ephemeral, and YouTube's hosting platform is no different. The existence of this kind of archive for Hmong micro media content is extremely rare, as very few Hmong media outlets have the resources to store, organize, or provide access to materials (Lopez 2018). For all minority media outlets, the combination of limited output and representation of a marginalized perspective means that archives are particularly important, as we will discuss further in chapter 5.

The audience for Hmong YouTube videos also engages with these digital collections of videos in particular ways that must be understood as different from broadcast television, as well as other digital platforms. For those with sufficient literacy (both in written language and the ability to navigate technological interfaces), YouTube's affordances allow users to participate in a range of activities, including requesting notifications of recently added content through subscriptions, creating playlists of videos or watching playlists created by others, participating in up-voting or down-voting videos, and engaging in dialogue with users by commenting on videos. But if we return to the story of Mee, a more recent Hmong American refugee with limited literacy skills, we must also consider the significant role that algorithms play in shaping how users encounter different content—rather than assuming that every user is able to wield control of the platform using all of the affordances that are technically available. Channels like 3HMONGTV, Suab Hmong News, and Hmong TV 24 Hours provide many of the top hits when users search for terms like "Hmong news" and "Hmong tv." On YouTube, "flow" is created through the platform's recommendation algorithm, which chooses videos that automatically play as soon as a video concludes. This affordance helps users with all levels of literacy (including children) enjoy the platform and its endless archive of content while also introducing elements that cannot be easily controlled or programmed to benefit channel owners.

In some homes I visited, technologically proficient family members knew how to cast the content from an iPad or laptop onto a flat-screen television set in the living room. This meant that less technologically proficient individuals could enjoy the larger screen and have the shared experience of viewing content with multiple family members at once. This physical setup generally promotes more of a "hands-off" viewing experience in comparison to the high-touch experience of individually clicking through a handheld device or laptop. In the absence of a remote control that can be used to "channel surf" through the array of videos, many viewers simply allowed the YouTube algorithm to auto-play.

The powerful role of YouTube's algorithm in moving users through and across different content can both harm and benefit Hmong video news outlets. In a previous study of the Asian American YouTube channel ISAtv (Lopez 2017), I discuss the way that YouTube users rely on the logic of television when they create channels populated with clearly differentiated and regularly updated programs. These channels are then in competition with one another for views and need to engage in effective branding practices in an attempt to stop users from "changing the channel." I argue that when Asian Americans and other minorities fail to sufficiently differentiate their brand from other YouTube channels, it helps to collectively raise the profile of the all Asian American YouTubers by reifying a commodity audience that is interested very broadly in Asian American content. The same principle can be seen at work here with Hmong YouTube channels, as YouTube's algorithms may move users from one Hmong news channel to another with little preference for any specific brand—an outcome that collectively supports Hmong YouTubers. Indeed, when I asked Mee and other Hmong YouTube users if they had a favorite news channel, they rarely were able to name any specific channel or host. They also had no knowledge of the production conditions that supported any of the news videos they watched, and thus could not distinguish between micro news outlets that only existed digitally and traditional news outlets that were supported by extensive paid staff and originally broadcast on network television stations. Users like Mee simply went to YouTube for Hmong content, and were pleased by the proliferation of new videos that helped them to feel updated and connected to a broader Hmong community across the internet.

This lack of preference for specific news outlets and reliance on algorithmic video selection has multiple impacts—it may collectively benefit the diverse array of Hmong videographers on YouTube by raising their visibility, but professional news outlets might benefit individually from seeking out more control and predictability. Mitch Lee noted that 3HMONGTV currently uploads entire programs to its YouTube channel so that it can grow its viewership, but his ultimate goal is to funnel his audience to the website and mobile app. These proprietary spaces can be considered digital enclosures (Andrejevic 2007) as they allow users to access content for free while also collecting data about user choices and patterns. This kind of surveillance, coupled with the stickiness of a branded space that decreases the likelihood of "changing the channel," is extremely valuable to micro media entrepreneurs. But as with so many financial and technological challenges facing these individuals, they must currently make do with the free platforms that are currently available to them—and that are sufficiently serving their audiences, who are enthusiastic for any and all content.

Power and Participation

This ecological approach to Hmong video news organizations has revealed the movement of content across many different platforms and technologies—including the websites of news outlets, YouTube, and mobile apps. One of the similarities across each platform is the maintenance of a professional aesthetic and discourse that strive to uphold the dominance and power of the media entrepreneur and their media corporation. This includes the use of visual conventions that evoke mainstream video news productions, as well as the construction of a corporate identity (Boyd 2001). This corporate identity relies on organizational rhetoric that distinguishes a corporation from its individual owner and helps to establish the legitimacy of Hmong micro media outlets. For instance, owners often use the term "we" when talking about their own decisions (e.g., "We at Suab Hmong Broadcasting") and terms like "headquarters" and "network" that imply a certain size and scale.

The struggle for media power is not unique to Hmong media entrepreneurs; media have long been recognized as a powerful force in our lives—shaping our daily experiences, contributing to our concept of ourselves and our realities, and facilitating connections to our communities. As such, those who control the media also wield power within society more broadly. Yet as Nick Couldry (2000) argues, we must also consider the ways in which the power media holds is largely symbolic, and thus tenuous, demanding continual reinforcement and negotiation. This is particularly the case within a changing media landscape, as new and emerging forms of media jostle one another for primacy amid a lively landscape of media choices.

While there have been many examinations of the symbolic power that is accorded to mainstream media institutions, we must also ask about the construction of power for minority communities who have limited access to media production. Indeed, the Hmong diasporic media landscape is relatively flat in comparison to the massively disproportionate power of, for instance, American network television and international multimedia conglomerates versus the media produced by everyday citizens on social media. We have seen throughout this book that Hmong media are dominated by volunteer-run outlets characterized by a high degree of volatility and personal risk. Within this context, moments of instability and rupture are particularly meaningful as media outlets without institutional longevity or significant financial capital can be vulnerable. Micro media outlets are also particularly vulnerable to changing directions or shuttering completely due to the extremely compact organizational structure that relies heavily on the individual owner's sustained interest and enthusiasm in the project.

In order to assess the way that different media platforms and technologies contribute to media power for Hmong micro media entrepreneurs, we can expand our ecological approach to include other forms of media that engage with, comment on, and potentially impact Hmong news organizations. This section will focus on a specific incident where one of the Hmong digital news networks was criticized for a story that it aired and led to an outpouring of conversation on social media and even mainstream media outlets. In analyzing this magnified media event that is rich with cultural significance, we can see the struggle for control and power by micro media entrepreneurs in the face of a participatory digital culture that increasingly allows for media audiences to have a say in the way that media are produced and what it conveys.

Responses to *Poj Niam Tsis Zoo*

In July 2015, Hmong TV 24 Hours posted a video called "Hmong TV #1 *Poj Niam Tsis Zoo* (Bad Women)." The thirteen-minute video features Doua Chialy Her (using his stage name "Doua Chialy") speaking directly to camera from behind his news desk. He discusses the way that many Hmong men have had their lives ruined by divorce and criticizes divorced women. He says that the women are fully to blame for divorce, and claims that divorced women are worthless: "Since you have fallen into the category of a divorced woman, I want you to change yourself and that you are the one in fault for not listening to your husband, not doing what is good for your husband's legacy and you only want to do it your way is why you are a divorcee. . . . You women who are divorced have also fallen into the category of trash. What does that mean? It means that you are bad, crooked, a no good and that you do not take care of your husband." He also advocates for divorced men who marry new younger wives from Laos because their previous wives argued too much and asked for a divorce. His openly misogynistic claims attempt to preserve traditional gender roles in the face of cultural change and a growing movement for Hmong women's rights and gender equality.

The response to this video was swift, as viewers immediately began to articulate their criticism and anger. The first wave of comments showed up on the YouTube video itself, as the site allows for text comments to be posted below each individual video. Another heavily circulated form of immediate commentary was a response video posted to YouTube by a Hmong American male artist and activist named Tou Ger Bennett Xiong. In the video, Xiong opens with a four-minute clip of Her's comments, and then proceeds with his own commentary in a mix of Hmong and English. He wears a bright blue T-shirt and shoots from a domestic location, presumably his own home. The backdrop visible in the frame includes a messy computer desk covered in papers and a bulletin board covered with photographs and cards. He says: "Your words have really touched my heart in a negative way. You label all the women, you blame them, you shame them, you embarrass them, and you say it is all their fault. As a Hmong man, you are not a man." Some of his speech is calm and seems prepared, but in other moments he becomes overwhelmed by emotion and passion. While Her represents the power of the professional journalist and media entrepreneur, Xiong visually evokes the presentation style of popular YouTubers. He represents a more youthful and modern version of Hmong masculinity. The genre of the "commentary video" helps Xiong's video to gain views and visibility since YouTube's algorithms will often auto-play "related videos" or otherwise guide viewers of the original video toward Xiong's response by highlighting it in the sidebar.

Within days, Her removed his offending video from YouTube. In response to the elimination of a direct space for communication and debate about the video, users simply migrated to other online platforms. Individuals and Hmong community organizations posted links to the video on their Facebook walls along with their own criticisms and commentary, and wrote blog posts. Another response was the creation of an online petition hosted at Change.org called "Public Apology" (2015). Created by a user named Paris Xiong, the petition is addressed to "Doua Chialy" and "Hmong TV." It includes an English translation of Chialy's speech in the form of bullet points, and then asks people to sign the petition "so that Hmong women, whether single, married, divorced, or widowed get some respect in our Hmong community and so men like Doua Chialy understand that we are humans too. We are not property, we are not garbage, and we are not disposable." It garnered over 2,800 signatures and was widely shared on Facebook and other social media platforms. A month later the conversation was still ongoing, and Minnesota Public Radio journalist Doualy Xaykaothao published a radio program and online news story about the controversy (Xaykaothao 2015). Xaykaothao focused on the cultural context surrounding Her's comments, giving voice to Hmong community members who were offended because Hmong women already experience so much unfair blame and social punishment.

These messages that address a specific Hmong television outlet in a moment of heightened scrutiny help us to understand what Hmong micro media outlets mean to audiences. With regard to this specific debate within the Hmong community, it helps us to see the centrality of contemporary gender roles and the shifting norms around marriage within Hmong American culture. Indeed, there are dozens of Hmong American organizations, associations, nonprofits, publications, and informal groups that are centered on the topic of addressing gender inequality, gender justice, and changing gender norms in Hmong society.[1] Yet we also gain insight into how audiences interpret the business practices of Hmong TV 24 Hours in relation to its social role. They clearly believe that the network has an ethical responsibility to the Hmong public it serves, as we can see in this public message that was posted on Facebook by a Hmong women's rights collective: "As a news outlet for many who do not have access to other in-language programs, Hmong TV should have higher standards for its staff and representatives . . . we find it unacceptable that Hmong TV even allowed it in the first place." Members of this community are angry because he is supposed to represent Hmong TV, and position the consequences for his actions at the level of the media outlet itself. They focus on the fact that Hmong audiences have so few media outlets to turn to, and this is why each individual outlet should strive to help Hmong people. This argument about the scarcity of media outlets is one of the reasons behind the FCC's fairness doctrine, a national policy that required public broadcasters to address controversial issues in an equitable and balanced way. Since 1949, it gave the government power to deny broadcast licenses to stations that did not give airtime to a diversity of perspectives. It was struck down in 1987 by opponents who argued that it unfairly restricted free speech and that the expansion of media outlets meant there were plenty of opportunities for a diversity of perspectives. Within the arena of Hmong media, there is clearly a concern that the limited availability of options (even when turning to digital outlets) means that each individual voice still carries a disproportionate amount of power.

Moreover, this history of media regulation continues to shape the way that many audiences believe media should continue to be held accountable. Many Hmong commenters on the Change.org petition appealed to the expectation that the FCC is responsible for making sure public media adheres to a set of community standards, and categorized Hmong TV 24 Hours as a broadcast television station that would fall under its jurisdiction: "I am proud that our Hmong women have come out of their usual humility and voice their dissent and disapproval of the way Hmong TV's handling of this matter and have instigated a public sanction and condemnation of Doua Chialy's demeanor and the Hmong TV who harbors such coward behavior unbecoming of a public station. I further motion that Hmong TV's broadcast license be suspended until the station has come up with some remedy or status change." As Hmong TV 24 Hours is an all-digital outlet, it does not require a broadcast license that could be suspended, and cannot be considered a "public station." These messages also reveal the assumption that Her's individual voice is actually representative of a larger media entity and organization comprised of staff and representatives who might have oversight over what is said on the station. The realities of Hmong television as a micro media industry are elided in the comments above, as well as others like this one posted to the Change.org petition:

"I'm not sure who to be upset with. The TV station and producers or the guy himself. Obviously, everyone was in on it. We should take the TV station down." We can see that Hmong TV 24 Hours is understood as a professional "TV station" that has different levels of supervision and a distinction between different decision-making bodies. Audiences assume that as a television station, there are collective professional bodies who participate in making decisions like hiring news anchors or greenlighting discussion topics. In calling attention to these misunderstandings, I am not trying to show the ignorance of the commenters or to denigrate the status of all-digital content providers. Rather, these comments help to reveal some of the shared assumptions about the role of the media in society, the way that micro media industries maintain power, and the way that these assumptions and responsibilities shape the role of micro media entrepreneurs.

This framing of Her's video as being equivalent to broadcast television is also upheld in the Minnesota Public Radio news article about the controversy. In the lede to her article, reporter Doualy Xaykaothao describes Her as "a St. Paul talk-show host who calls himself the Hmong Jerry Springer." While this comment is neutrally stated without any comment on what it might mean or whether or not it is an apt comparison, this self-description that compares Her to an American talk show superstar serves to bolster the connection. Indeed, it reminds readers that reckless, bold, and controversial forms of televisual masculinity have always been at the heart of American television. If this is the mode in which Her seeks to operate, there may be no need for decorum and respectability.

Among the hundreds of comments on the Change.com petition, there is only one that demonstrates a clear understanding of how the Hmong TV 24 Hours outlet operates: "This is his own TV show, so he can advertise his business products, this Hmong TV is belong to him. no body hire him to do. that's why he think he can say any thing that he wanted to say [sic]." Although the person who wrote this comment ostensibly signed the petition in the hopes that outside pressure might still convince Her to apologize, this comment nevertheless pulls back the curtain on the realities of the video and why he may not. Indeed, the lack of regulation, oversight, or need for advertisers effectively means that micro media industries like Hmong TV 24 Hours have the freedom to do whatever they please. Indeed, Her showed little remorse for his comments. The next video that he posted was ostensibly an apology, but it was criticized by Xiong on the Change.org petition as doing "the complete opposite," with Her merely defending his previous statements. Her also invited Hmong women to join him on later videos, and they largely defended him.

This incident reveals the power that micro media outlets can wield, the way that power is perceived by community members, and how negotiations and attempts to shift that power can take place. Audiences of this micro media outlet clearly recognize Hmong TV 24 Hours as legitimate, and see the media entrepreneur at its helm as a powerful member of their community because of the public platform he controls. This is not to say that all micro-staffed You-Tube channels can post recklessly without any fear of negative consequences. Amid the rise of elite YouTube creators who are making six-figure incomes, we have seen a number of YouTubers who have been forced to apologize for their mistakes. Some high-profile examples of this include video game vlogger PewDiePie apologizing for using the N-word during a video game, comedian Logan Paul apologizing for making light of a suicide death, beauty vlogger Laura Lee apologizing for racist tweets, and travel vlogger RiceGum apologizing for insulting comments about Chinese people eating dogs. While these individual videographers cannot be pressured to respond to criticism by You-Tube or any other regulatory or legal body, they do respond to outrage from their fans due to a specific kind of influence—each of these videographers command substantial ad revenues based on their popularity, so their financial revenues will be decreased if they lose followers. They make money through the Google AdSense program that rewards channel owners for views and subscriptions, as well as through brand ads, selling merchandise, affiliate links, and other mechanisms that demand audience quantities and engagement. While this means that audiences can sometimes have power over even media outlets run by just one person, it also means that audiences have more influence when that outlet is extremely popular and dependent on maintaining a massive fan base. The cultivation of a happy and constantly growing body of loyal viewers is important to media outlets of all sizes, but is certainly less critical for outlets that already traffic in relatively small numbers.

There may be limits to the power of flak in convincing a YouTube news outlet to apologize or change its ways, but if we return to our ecological understanding of the Hmong media landscape we can still see opportunities for participation and polyvocality. Indeed, in the previous chapter's discussion of newspapers, the letters to the editor page often served as a key battleground for debates about Hmong news because there were so few other ways for the community to speak back. With the emergence of digital platforms and their uptake in the Hmong community, there are now a multitude of opportunities for audiences to voice their perspectives—and, more importantly, to organize collective responses in a way that makes most sense to participants.

Indeed, a meaningful response of this kind came from a collective of women on the Facebook page of an organization called Hmong Women Today. The community of more than nine thousand women also comes together in person for events such as women's retreats, networking meetups, and cultural summits. Two days after Doua Chialy posted his video, the organization posted a message calling for their Facebook followers to send a "#Proud #Selfie" and a mini-bio. The call was originally created by Kabo Yang, who was quoted in the

Hmong Times: "In response to negative and remarks degrading and objectifying women, I felt the need to change and expand the way Hmong women are perceived . . . to unite and build a force against fear and intimidation" (May 16, 2016). Over fifty women responded and posted photographs of themselves alongside stories of their inspirations and their successes in life—including earning college degrees, taking up a wide variety of professions, and becoming wives and mothers. For example, one post read: "I am a proud Hmong daughter, wife and mother to a beautiful baby girl. At a young age, I witnessed many Hmong women struggle with achieving a higher education and with their careers. As a result, I have mentored many young Hmong women and men to achieving a higher education, as well as working hard to obtained [*sic*] my nursing degree at only 18 years old. I went on to work as Trauma/Surgical ICU nurse, and obtained my Master of Science in Nursing Educational Leadership." Each post contains hashtags such as #HmongWomenStandUp, #IAmHmong-Woman, #HmongWomenStand2GetherOnly, and #HmongWomenToday. While the posts are consistently upbeat in framing their successes and personal journeys, some include stories of struggle and the difficulties they have faced as Hmong women. One woman wrote, "Though my first marriage didn't succeed I didn't let the criticism from the Hmong community shatter my future. I knew my life had a purpose and I was determined to live because I knew I was worthy." Another wrote, "My parents divorced when I was 4, and I was raised by my grandparents for most years of my life. I was once told that growing up in a Hmong family meant I was going to become a high school drop out and get pregnant at a young age. Little did they know, what they said to me actually became my biggest motivation." Together the stories, photos, and hashtags clearly serve to put forward a counter-narrative about who Hmong women are and the positive role they play in shaping Hmong culture. Rather than directly trying to censor or condemn Doua Chialy Her's original message, they simply used their own digital platform to create a counter-message and targeted it their Hmong women followers.

Both the Change.org petition and Facebook hashtag campaign disregard journalistic rituals and other normalized practices for gaining media power. But they are also different from the video response posted to YouTube by Tou Ger Bennett Xiong that was described earlier. In contrast to the YouTube videos made by these two Hmong men, the strategies taken up by Hmong women downplay the voice of any one individual in favor of highlighting the strength of the collective. The Change.org petition aggregates names and comments, while the hashtag campaign broadcasts dozens of smiling faces and triumphant biographies. Together, these forms of media facilitate a response that shows the error of Her's arguments through the overwhelming number of those who disagree with him, generating a kind of media power through aggregation, rather than through individual celebrity or the establishment of journalistic authority.

Conclusion: Media Power in a Micro Media Ecology

This analysis of the Hmong television landscape has revealed the specific struggles that small communities face in developing their own television networks, which are traditionally supported by local advertising and professional staff. One of their innovations has been to develop online video platforms that emulate the look and professionalism of cable news channels, hailing Hmong audiences who prefer the digital enclave of YouTube to the barrage of English language programming on American television. Entrepreneurs in this digital space utilize many of the same strategies as the newspaper owners profiled in the previous chapter—cultivating multiple skill sets so that they can take over every aspect of media production and distribution, and developing a number of different media outlets to build a micro media empire. Together with the findings from the previous chapter, we can see the power of these outlets in the responses from their audiences who credit them with playing an important social role for their community and strive to hold them accountable. In both chapters, micro media entrepreneurs remain remarkably resilient in refusing to acquiesce to the demands of their audience—though this is particularly true for Hmong television networks that do not rely on advertising dollars to support their production. With business models that are dependent on a micro form of conglomeration that produces a transmedia complex of interconnected outlets, each individual outlet can withstand a greater amount of flak. The individual at the helm retains near-total control over every decision, including what stories to cover and how to cover them, in addition to many others, and does not necessarily need to placate their audience.

As we can see in the examples discussed so far, this level of control can have many different consequences—micro media entrepreneurs can be persistent advocates for justice in calling attention to stories from their community that might otherwise be ignored, and they can also use their media outlets to affirm already existing power dynamics and attack community members who are already vulnerable. Given that neither media producers nor audiences have a monopoly on integrity or justice, there is no inherent value to acquiescing to the demands of an irate audience. But this exploration of the controversy surrounding the *Poj Niam Tsis Zoo* story does help us to see how audiences set expectations for media in accordance with the norms of legacy media like television networks when they do not understand the realities of micro media entrepreneurship. When community members came together to voice their criticism of programming aired on Hmong TV 24 Hours, their comments reflected an assumption that this professional entity obeyed the same code of ethics, regulations, and responsibilities as mainstream television and broadcast stations. In contrast, writers in the letters to the editor section of Hmong newspapers showed that they did understand that one person was largely responsible for the entire outlet, and were able to express their needs and demands in ways that shaped how the outlet evolved.

The next chapter examines another kind of hybrid media platform that relies on digital technologies to produce a form of mass media that is low cost and easily accessible to Hmong audiences. Yet rather than relying on one media entrepreneur with multiple skill sets to produce all of the media content, it takes on the distinctively digital mode of user-generated content—enlisting the participation of a large number of people to get involved and share their voices. As we will see, the format I call "Hmong teleconference radio" offers a very different version of micro media that is deeply participatory and has the potential to greatly diversify the narratives that are propagated. Yet there are also numerous challenges that come with this kind of openness, both for its owners and those who participate in it.

4

Global Participatory
Networks

•

Teleconference Radio
Programs

Choua Lee's passion for teaching radiates through every aspect of her life. During the day, she teaches Hmong language to college students at the local university. On her drive home from work and during quiet moments at home, she often turns on her Facebook Live video to share musings about life and impart wisdom to her friends and community members. And every Sunday night from 8 to 10 P.M. she hosts a radio program centered on the topic of health and maintaining a healthy lifestyle. She carefully conducts research in advance so she can have a clear message that her listeners can trust, but she also aims to make all of her lessons approachable and fun. When eight o'clock rolls around, she picks up her cell phone and dials into a large, multiuser conference call. A robotic voice intones, "There are 1,340 participants on this call." Taking a deep breath, she launches into her show's intro. For the next two hours, she doles out advice, facilitates conversation among the other callers, and listens intently through her Bluetooth headset.

This activity of calling into a hosted conference call was one of the most popular kinds of media engagement with the Hmong Americans I spoke to. It goes by many different names, including "Hmong radio," "teleconference programs," and "cell phone shows," but here I use the term "Hmong teleconference radio" to describe the format that dominated my conversations with

Hmong Americans throughout the period of study. This form of radio is accessed through placing a phone call, either through a cell phone or a landline, and entering into a massive conference call. Using the kind of audio conference call software traditionally used by businesses, these open forums for aural communication are used to produce 24/7 live content for listeners. Free conference call platforms can host thousands of participants at a time; although all of the participants and programs studied here are based in the United States, the audiences for these programs extend throughout the global diaspora of Hmong—including those in Laos, Thailand, Australia, France, and other countries in which there are sizable Hmong populations (Lopez 2016).

The rise of this unique hybrid media platform that blends telephony and radio reflects the strength of Hmong oral culture and the long history of radio as a culturally resonant medium for Hmong communities. Just as low levels of literacy make video news programs more attractive to many Hmong Americans than print media such as newspapers, radio and other audio media are desirable due to their accessibility for those with low literacy. This chapter begins with an exploration of the history of Hmong radio of all formats—including weekly programs on community radio stations, as well as the rise of Hmong-owned stations on both the standard AM/FM dial and alternative outlets like low-power and subchannels. I then dive into Hmong teleconference radio programs, investigating their unique structure as well as the cultural context in which they intervene. Through interviews with four program owners, six hosts/DJs, and dozens of listeners, I explore what kinds of conversations are taking place on the programs, who participates in them, and how they are perceived by audiences. Like the forms of television that take place entirely on YouTube, this form of radio that takes place entirely on cell phones shows the way that small communities are utilizing new media technologies in ways that challenge mediated boundaries. In particular, it shows how micro media industries are well positioned to accommodate the specific needs of marginalized communities—in this case, the desire for a wide range of oral/aural media, and the need for accessibility via mobile phones that lack internet capabilities—through innovation and entrepreneurship.

The chapter then turns to the role of gender in shaping both the development of this format and what it means to Hmong communities. The powerful role that Hmong women are playing in initiating and sustaining this new space for communication serves to elevate the voices of some Hmong women and is beginning to change the shape of communication in the Hmong diaspora. Yet this accomplishment has not been easy or uncontested. I also uncover a deep suspicion and criticism of the shows—including condemnation of the intimate and emotional tenor of conversations, the lack of professionalization and regulation, and the ethos of participation and polyvocality that often contributes to conflict and cultural negotiation. Together with gendered understandings of mediated communication, unpaid labor, and telephony, I argue that these critiques must be understood as reflective of the same patriarchal inequalities that have long oppressed women and women-centered media. As a result, Hmong teleconference radio programs are often not regarded as a legitimate form of mass media or media industry, and the women who play a leadership role in this innovative cultural form are not recognized as communication leaders. This investigation of Hmong teleconference radio shows the way that micro media industries can offer possibility for marginalized and vulnerable members of the community to utilize innovative forms of labor and entrepreneurship to create a thriving counter-public. Yet it also shows how traditionally gendered hierarchies of value can minimize or altogether obscure this form of labor and its contributions.

Earliest Hmong Radio Programs on Community Radio

Some of the earliest forms of Hmong radio were through local community radio stations that were open to creating a slot for weekly Hmong outreach programs. With a tradition of welcoming participation from diverse populations, volunteer-run community radio stations have a mandate that centrally focuses on giving voice to community members and promoting democratic participation. Starting in 1985, one such program called *Hmong Public Radio* came on the air in Green Bay, Wisconsin. The channel WHID 88.1 FM reached a radius of 150 miles around Green Bay, and started to post playlists for Hmong Public Radio online in 2010. The program was the result of a collaboration between University of Wisconsin–Green Bay and the Catholic diocese. Host Jouabee Lor was the creator of the program, and husband-wife team Shoua Thao and Katie Thao took over in 2009 along with two other couples. Their program was hosted entirely in Hmong and ran for two hours a week, 5 P.M. to 7 P.M. Saturdays, with music, news, and educational information until it ended in 2016.

Similar programs also started popping up in other areas with large Hmong populations, such as the Twin Cities. *Hmong Wameng Radio Program* and the *Hmong American Reachout Program* were established on the community radio station KFAI 90.3 FM in Minneapolis. One of the first hosts was Shoua Xiong in 1986, who volunteered for Hmong Wameng Radio Program. Then in 1990, he proposed a new program called *Hmong American Reachout Program* and it was approved by the station's programming committee. The show is all in Hmong language. For the first thirty minutes Xiong plays traditional Hmong songs, and the last thirty minutes are held in talk show format along with his partners from Hmong American Partnership. In this segment, they address a number of different issues in the community including domestic violence prevention, health disparity issues, education, and Hmong history. The show is on every Sunday from 1 to 2 P.M., and an MP3 file of the week's show is posted online at the KFAI website. As discussed in chapter 2, Kathy Mouache-upao proposed another English language Hmong program called *HmongFM* on the same channel in 2006. Together with her brother Wameng Moua, publisher of the *Hmong Today* newspaper, they created an English language program that focused on Hmong American arts and news until 2017.

Since 1990, community radio station WORT 89.9 FM in Madison, Wisconsin, has also had a weekly program in Hmong language. The show was started by Kao Xiong and includes Hmong music, news, and interviews. In the early days, the show was only thirty minutes and the music recordings were on reel-to-reel or cassette tapes, often recordings from the refugee camps. Station manager Norm Stockwell asked if they might want to have a show in English, but the listeners said that there was plenty of English-language programming available and what they needed was news in their own language. In 1997 they requested to expand the show to an hour, and in 2002 to two hours. At the time of this research in 2018, the show was being run by a team of three to four different participants, including Pao Yang, who discusses Hmong American youth issues.

In Sheboygan, Xia Vue Yang has hosted a weekly Hmong language radio program since 1982. It airs on WSHS 91.7 FM, a student-run high school radio and public radio station. Yang first became interested in radio when he heard that Hmong parents were having a hard time learning about what was going on in the school district with their children. He was originally given a five-minute spot on the Sheboygan-area radio station WKTS every Sunday from 7:55 to 8:00 A.M. to make announcements in Hmong. Then he paid for an additional ten minutes for a total of fifteen minutes, but it still did not seem like enough. At that point, Yang learned about the high school radio station owned by the Sheboygan Area School District that was not in use during the evenings, and asked if he could use it for Hmong broadcasts. He started with sixty minutes every Thursday, and eventually grew to the entire evening from 3:30 to 10 P.M. In the early days, he would mentor high school students who wanted to volunteer for the radio show. But fewer and fewer students were interested in radio programming, and eventually he began running it on his own.

Every Sunday, from 7 to 8 A.M., Hmong Americans in La Crosse can tune in to WIZM 1410 AM for a current news and cultural affairs broadcast in the Hmong language. Since 2015, staff members from the La Crosse Area Hmong Mutual Assistance Association have broadcast a mixture of public service announcements, news, and community stories. They also file an English language translation at the station. There is also a one-hour Hmong show on WXCO 1230 AM out of Wasau. The show is produced by the Wausau Area Hmong Mutual Association and airs from 7 to 8 A.M. on Sundays.

These programs on community radio stations perform the important political function of inserting Hmong voices onto radio stations that otherwise cater to non-Hmong audiences, and in doing so, acknowledge Hmong Americans as part of their local communities. They also offer the security and consistent support of a larger station. Yet with their limited length—ranging from one hour to a handful of hours every week—such programs are an inadequate resource for Hmong American audiences. This is particularly the case for those who rely on these programs for news, as we might imagine that there are far more important news items in a given week than can be covered in a single hour.

Hmong-Owned AM/FM Radio Stations

To address these limits and provide more consistent content, many Hmong Americans have sought to own their own AM/FM radio stations. This has not been easy, as purchasing an entire radio facility is often prohibitively expensive and the paperwork filing with the FCC is arduous. Although California's Central Valley has the largest population of Hmong in the United States at over 75,000, Hmong radio has been rare. From 2005 to 2010, Hmong Americans in Fresno leased the radio station KQEQ 1210 AM, but in 2018 when I surveyed the landscape there was only one radio station with a focus on Hmong programming—KBIF 900 AM. The programming at KBIF is primarily Hmong focused, but the station is owned by Gore-Overgaard Broadcasting and is managed by president Tony Donato, who is non-Hmong. KBIF also prominently features Punjabi language music and programming. Both the Hmong and Punjabi content are brokered by the hour to the individuals who are responsible for them. This means that community members can pay to do their own show, and then they are responsible for acquiring advertisers if they want financial support for their program. Donato describes what this untraditional format means:

> We offer our station to anyone who wants to do a radio show. Before we used to sell it to anybody—mainly religious, and then weekends and evenings would go to other groups. We're selling you an hour of real estate. You're brokering that hour, now that's your hour to do whatever you want, as long as it's within our guidelines. You pay us for that hour, you can sub it out to anyone as far as advertising. It's not traditional. Because when you have a station, you want to format it yourself and get advertising dollars. But this format will only work for so long. If you don't have numbers, a lot of agencies will buy agencies that have big numbers, so they won't place their client's dollars on that station.

The station is too small to be rated by Arbitron, and they know that language barriers can make it difficult to survey their listeners in order to learn more about them. In the early days of the station, programming included a mix of religious content and an extremely wide array of ethnic programming—at one point, featuring programming in eleven different languages, only one of which was Hmong. Yet the Hmong programming quickly became popular and reliable, growing from one evening a week to five evenings a week. Advertisers in the area were also interested in reaching the Hmong community, so the station slowly started shifting its priorities toward Hmong content on the weekdays. The same was true for Punjabi content, which had come to dominate the weekends. Their Hmong lineup now includes plenty of time for both traditional and contemporary Hmong music, as well as a buy-sell-trade hour that serves as Hmong classified ads, talk shows and interviews, and programming focusing on Generation X.

While KBIF is able to provide a steady stream of Hmong content in spite of its non-Hmong ownership, there are also three stations in the Midwest that are entirely Hmong owned and operated. Peter Xiong has been the owner and manager of KPNP 1600 AM in St. Paul since 2006. Prior to KPNP, he and Kor Xiong and another partner owned a subchannel from an FM signal, but they split ways to take on their own independent projects. Peter Xiong had a passion for radio since his first day in the United States, and wanted to create one of the first Hmong-owned stations. He explained to me in an interview that his love for radio emerged from his experiences in Laos: "Radio came to my mind because during 1961 to 1975, there was a Hmong radio station in Laos that Americans made for them. It was shut off completely in May 1975, it may have been destroyed. I got into this country in 1987 and came directly to Minneapolis, and my goal is to get a radio station. I wanted it to tell the truth, get rid of rumors in the community from uneducated people. I like to tell people the truth." He started training with KFAI to learn about radio programming. In 2006, he bought KPNP from a Spanish language station at the call sign KZGX. Peter Xiong is proud that the station is Hmong owned and centers Hmong voices, particularly given that all over the world there is a dearth of Hmong radio. He traveled to China, Laos, Thailand, and Burma to research Hmong radio, and could only find instances of government-owned radio stations that allowed Hmong to speak for an hour or two per day. The slogan for Minority Radio KPNP is "The Gateway to the Minority Community in Minnesota and the World." Its mission is to serve the thousands of underserved minority community members living in the Minneapolis metropolitan area through creating a multicultural radio station.

In 2014, the station KFXN 690 AM in St. Paul was purchased by Kongsue Xiong and Xeng Xiong. Their journey to ownership started thirteen years earlier, when Kongsue purchased an NPR affiliate's subcarrier station, a Subsidiary Communications Authorization (SCA) signal designed for minorities. In order to tune into the station, listeners had to purchase special receivers and remain in their homes. Others told him that the venture would fail, but he made connections with radio hosts in Thailand and Laos and was able to rebroadcast their international programming. He also worked on developing his own skills as an educator and community leader, enjoying the opportunity to help his Hmong community better their lives.

Then he set his sights on KFXN, which at the time was a local sports station. It was acquired by Clear Channel for $1.4 million in 1998. But after only one year, Clear Channel donated the station for tax deduction purposes to the Minority Media and Telecommunications Council (MMTC). Kongsue Xiong was able to run the station under a local marketing agreement starting in 2011, and then purchased the station in 2014. He explains:

> They looked at my application and saw my experience and they considered it. We had to exchange a lot of information, and show financial support. So we do all that and finally we had to fly to Washington DC to meet the guy and finish the business. It took about a year to finish. Even though we didn't have a lot of money, they leased to us first, so we could pay off. So thank you very much for MMTC that they were willing to get the funds for us temporarily. That was very positive, without them we cannot do anything.

The station's staff consists of only Kongsue Xiong and Xeng Xiong, who do all of the work along with occasional volunteers. He would like to hire more staff, and always envisioned his company supporting others who wanted to do radio. But they can only afford to pay contractors with trades for service or giving time to advertise their businesses.

A third Hmong-owned radio station is Hmong Radio WIXK 1590 AM, which expanded to also broadcast from an FM translator on 103.3 FM. It is owned by Mai Yia Yang, who purchased the station in 2014. Mai Yia Yang stood out within Hmong radio because she is the only female owner, and it was this lack of women in the radio industry that inspired her to get involved. She explains, "At first, I just looked at the big picture of radio and there's a lot of radio out there, and especially a lot of men. A lot of men own it. But maybe women can own it too, which is the way I look at it. There's not a Hmong woman own it yet. At first I thought, am I gonna make it? Are people going to feel the same way as people feel about other people who own radio? But it's a passion. Sometimes I feel like being on radio is like therapy for me." She set out to fill what she perceived as a gap in Hmong radio—music and programming that would appeal to younger Hmong Americans. On her own show, she tries to play all new music, rather than the old familiar classics that appeal mostly to the elders. She also seeks to expand her audience by including some programming in English. Yang describes her reasons for this:

> This station is a little bit different from other stations I guess. When we talk, anything that comes out of your mouth is ok—English, Hmong, whatever. As

long as people understand and we don't violate FCC, it's ok. We mix everything, it's fine. This radio station is for the generation right now, and you don't need to be pure Hmong to talk. We've got to move to a new generation, pull all the youth and the new generation in. I don't mean it to isolate the elders, but you know, let's not focus too much on the elders. We do respect them, but we live in America in a new society, everything is different.

In addition to programs hosted by Yang, WIXK also has nearly a dozen volunteer hosts who each focus on their own topic or style of music. This includes the queer youth–oriented show *Nplooj*, which is discussed in detail in chapter 5.

Subchannels and Low-Power Radio Stations

While it can cost hundreds of thousands of dollars to purchase a station on the AM/FM spectrum, FM channels can carry a number of subchannels on their bandwidth. These digital subchannels are a way for the FM station to subdivide their data stream, producing additional broadcast channels that may vary in audio quality but cost much less money to purchase. As mentioned earlier, listeners access these SCA stations by purchasing an SCA radio receiver, such as those produced by MetroSonix that cost $45–$65 each. One such subchannel that provides Hmong programming 24/7 is Hmong Wisconsin Radio based out of Appleton. Owner Kor Xiong started the channel with some friends in 2004 in Minnesota, but then moved it to Wisconsin because the opportunity arose and they felt there was a need for Southeast Asian news in northeastern Wisconsin. It has three employees and is the only private, commercial radio station in Wisconsin for Hmong audiences.

Another option for producing and distributing radio at a lower cost is through low-power radio stations. There are at least two low-power radio stations leased to Hmong Americans, including WFNU in the Frogtown area of Minnesota and WNRB in Wausau. The studio for WFNU is in the Center for Hmong Arts and Talents, but the station is co-owned by a number of different nonprofit organizations and its DJs are primarily Black and Latinx. Their website shows that there is only one program that includes any Hmong content—a storytelling healthcare hour that serves the Somali, Latino, and Hmong communities. The station in Wausau has mostly Hmong programming on the weekend, run by volunteers from the Wausau Area Hmong Mutual Association. Throughout the week they have an assortment of English and Hmong programming.

The Teleconference Radio Format

While there are clearly many different ways that radio has come to populate the Hmong media ecology, these descriptions help to highlight the forces that limit the reach of Hmong radio in general. The high cost of purchasing an AM/ FM radio station has meant that the Twin Cities is the only geographic region with Hmong-owned stations, and those who live in every other region in the United States cannot turn on their car radio and hear Hmong voices. The low-cost alternatives are also imperfect—FM subchannels require audiences to purchase a piece of single-use technology, while the free programming available through community radio is limited to only a couple of hours a week. The invention of Hmong teleconference radio programs addresses both of these shortcomings, producing a free radio service with 24/7 programming that can be accessed from anywhere in the world. This kind of inventiveness is characteristic of micro media industries, which are well positioned to experiment with technological affordances in unique ways that address their target audiences and specific needs.

Although it is unclear when the first Hmong teleconference radio came into existence, most dated their emergence to around 2008 or 2009. There are two sociotechnological factors that allowed for their rise—the availability of free conference call platforms and the affordability of mobile phone plans with endless wireless minutes.[1] Mobile technologies are extremely common within Hmong American families, used to maintain interpersonal relationships with friends and relatives and generally share information about goings-on in the Hmong community. Cell phones are a relatively affordable and accessible communication technology that is easily utilized even by older Hmong Americans with low levels of English proficiency, literacy, or technological savvy. If the callers were being charged by the minute to participate or the shows were expensive to host, this would not be a sustainable form of mass communication for the same reasons that traditional broadcast and print media have struggled. But with the decline in using mobile phones to make voice calls, wireless plans with endless minutes are now affordable and commonplace (Bensinger 2012).

As a result, many participants describe their engagement with the programs in terms of long-term, daily usage—they call into the teleconference radio programs from the minute they wake up in the morning and remain connected throughout the day, often falling asleep to the sound of the radio programs at night. Others call in more sporadically, tuning in on occasion when they want to fill time while doing chores or relaxing after work. Callers either listen with the phone to their ear or put the phone on speakerphone so that the call is audible from a greater distance, which means that friends and family who are nearby can listen as well. There are some websites and other online forums that promote the shows, but most of the participants had learned about the call-in number from a family member or close friend. The use of conference call software to host these radio programs allows upward of two or three thousand participants to listen at the same time. The shows did not seem to fill to this capacity; most shows my research assistants listened to had between five hundred and one thousand current listeners, as announced by an automated voice at the start of the call.

While this platform does not have the industrial constraints placed on radio, Hmong teleconference radio is run in a way that is based on and extremely similar to traditional broadcast radio stations. There are dozens of different Hmong teleconference numbers that are accessible at any moment, each using its own unique call-in number and run by different individuals across the country. Each conference call owner is responsible for using conference call software on their computer to initiate the call, which we might consider a "station." The owner then manages the channel by scheduling DJs to serve as hosts throughout the day, and more generally shaping the mission and programming for the channel. DJs are assigned consistent blocks of time every week that they are in charge of facilitating. Each show lasts one to two hours and is centered on a specific topic, such as music/singing, health, relationships, youth issues, folktales, and many others. Just as the Hmong YouTube programs discussed in the previous chapter approximate televisual flow through their digital delivery platform, these radio programs deliver a recognizably "radio" flow to their listeners.

All of the conversations take place in Hmong language, using a blend of the White Hmong and Green Hmong dialects that are most common in the United States.[2] The entire staff is unpaid, given that the conference calls are free to own, operate, and participate in. But those in leadership positions take their role very seriously, particularly their goal of creating a forum for communication that is open to participants across the Hmong diaspora. One owner stated: "The overarching theme that we have is that we are not local, but rather on the cellphone waves and anyone can call and listen. It does not matter if you are young or old, you can call and listen. All you have to do is call the number and you are in. They can also speak up, communicate with others because we are not a listening show, we are a show where we can communicate with others." The owner's comments reveal that the participatory quality of the show is a deliberate feature, created in opposition to the one-way forms of communication that only allow for passive consumption. This forum is then able to facilitate connections between Hmong who are dispersed across the United States and the globe, many of whom otherwise possess limited access to the broader diasporic community, and invite them into this massive conversation with the mere touch of a button.

A Participatory Form of Radio

Hmong teleconference radio programs deploy many conventions from traditional radio, but their deeply participatory nature is one of the ways in which they challenge radio's norms. Traditional broadcast radio shows rely on the authoritative voice of a DJ who controls the flow of information or music. Even during designated call-in shows, which are common on traditional broadcasts, there are gatekeeping processes in place that screen callers and limit access to public participation (Dori-Hacohen 2012), and it is the interaction between the host and the caller that is the primary goal of the show. In contrast, one of the defining characteristics of Hmong teleconference radio is their polyvocality and the ease with which listeners can become speakers.

When participants call into one of the teleconference calls, they are first greeted with a message informing them of what number they must dial if they want to speak. The format of the shows is generally that they begin with the DJ introducing the designated topic for that hour, but the bulk of the conversation is collectively produced through the participation of those who call in— whether that is through callers performing a song, telling a folktale, giving advice about health, discussing current events, or holding forth on any number of topics of conversation. Although the host of the program and the owner have the ability to mute or kick out callers who do not follow the rules or conventions of the conference call space, the general feeling is that all participants are invited to speak up if they want to. If there are hundreds or thousands of listeners and only one person speaks at a time, it is certainly the case that the majority of participants are only listening. Yet this ethos of participation, where anyone who feels impassioned about a topic is invited to share their opinion, is one of the central markers of participatory culture. Participatory culture is defined by Henry Jenkins et al. (2006) as "a culture with relatively low barriers to artistic expression and civic engagement, strong support for creating and sharing one's creations, and some type of informal mentorship whereby what is known by the most experienced is passed along to novices. A participatory culture is also one in which members believe their contributions matter, and feel some degree of social connection with one another" (3). Beyond simply describing a relationship that participants have to one another, participatory cultures are important to note as such because of the benefits that they can provide. These include opportunities for learning and skill development, but also an increase in the potential for empowerment. In talking to those who own, host, call into, and listen to Hmong teleconference radio programs, it seems clear that this form of media is marked by participatory culture. This is an important distinction, given that the other forms of micro media analyzed thus far—including newspapers, television stations, and other video outlets—have been decidedly closed off to participation and limited to the contributions of the few entrepreneurs at the top. In examining a kind of micro media industry that is open to outside voices and relatively limited in its control over communication, we can then see how openness and loss of control become barriers that micro media industries are forced to overcome in order to gain legitimacy and respect from their niche audiences.

The participatory culture engendered within these programs can be better understood through looking at some of the specific formats, such as the singing shows that one participant spoke about as his favorite. He loved calling into programs where callers simply took turns singing Hmong songs, one after the other, until they grew tired of singing. He enjoyed these shows because they gave him the chance to interact with Hmong artists, to improve his singing based on feedback he received from fellow callers, and to make friends with those who helped him. This model of musical performance and co-creation challenges the top-down format of traditional radio, where privately owned corporations exercise direct control over what songs are broadcast over the airwaves, and listeners can only participate by passively listening. Within Hmong teleconference radio programs, participants have the opportunity to not only choose what songs are shared, but if they should so desire, they can perform the song themselves before thousands of listeners. Shows that focus on musical performance offer a clear example of participatory culture in the sense that Jenkins et al. elucidates, with a strong focus on sharing artistic expression and engendering a culture of mentorship and support for one's contributions. In the case of shows focused on traditional Hmong sung poetry or *kwv txhiaj*, this format can also help to keep a vital cultural tradition alive by encouraging new practitioners and providing a space for practicing and performing this challenging art form. Other Hmong teleconference radio programs dedicated to topics such as Hmong medicine or financial matters similarly invite callers to join into the conversation. The mantle of expertise is shared among the varied participants, each of whom are invited to take their turn voicing their own perspective.

Beyond sharing and sustaining cultural art forms, the interactive and flexible format of the shows open up a space for discussing what it means to be Hmong and how Hmong culture is changing. As with all ethnic media, such discussions can be seen to perform the ideological function of shaping Hmong identities and ways of life (Molina Guzman 2006). We can particularly see this in the titles of the shows, such as *Hmong in the 21st Century*, *Men and Women Nowadays*, and *If There is No Tomorrow*, which broadly address the way that Hmong people see themselves and their lives in relation to the past and the future. Other shows provide discussion forums for common struggles in the lives of Hmong all over the world, including the difficulties of growing up in poverty or being a young mother or young father, how to reduce stress, or how to deal with jealousy in relationships. These topics help us to understand the kinds of issues that are most interesting, provocative, or useful to Hmong listeners. By creating and participating in these conversations, Hmong people are creating an unregulated and nonhierarchical forum for communicating cultural norms, as well as for potentially shifting or challenging those norms.

The Geographic Reach of Hmong Participation

The participatory aspects of Hmong teleconference radio programs described here align with many of the values of community radio. As mentioned earlier, there are many forms of community media that are premised on openness and accessibility. This includes the community radio stations that allow Hmong radio hosts to have hourly programs for free, among others. While Hmong teleconference radio does build from these values, it also helps us expand on traditional understandings of community radio because of its global reach. Radio has traditionally been a distinctly local medium that is geographically circumscribed, and community radio in particular has denoted a physically connected community. Yet the Hmong programs analyzed here largely eschew any reference to local contexts and cannot be seen to promote mobilization around local issues. Rather, Hmong teleconference radio programs participate in interpellating and reifying a global Hmong diaspora. This is the "community" that the programs are designed to represent and bring together. We can see this framing in the description of one of the shows, as stated on their website: "[Friendship Radio] is a bridge, an echoing sound, a shining light, a powerful method for Hmong to send messages to one another. It doesn't matter where you are in the world, everyone will hear once the voices are made through this radio" (Vaj 2015). This global framing does not necessarily mean that the shows are consumed evenly across the Hmong diaspora or that they are accessible to Hmong all over the world. It is more accurate to describe the shows as being primarily centered in the United States, particularly given that all of the phone numbers used to access Hmong teleconference radio programs originate in the United States. Yet owners who can view statistics on the callers report that participants hail from a diverse array of countries, including many locations with large Hmong populations such as Thailand, Laos, France, and Australia.[3] Some participants also reported that their family members abroad called in to the shows, and those who had traveled to Laos confirmed that Hmong communities there were very familiar with the shows. More importantly, the shows are positioned as being for the "Hmong community"—a distinction that transcends local, regional, and national boundaries.

We can also better understand the spatial dimensions of the shows by looking at how conversations unfold on this platform. First, we can note the widespread use of anonymity for participants, with most speakers withholding their name or using a pseudonym—practices that can be seen to subvert attempts to identify individual participants within a specific location, community, or clan. Anonymity can partly be understood as a function of the aural nature of the programs, as the voice is often difficult to identify (Casillas 2011). Although Hmong participants in teleconference radio programs may not be seeking to avoid legal persecution, the veiling afforded by this solely aural medium is none-theless purposefully deployed to construct a safer environment for its partici-pants. Of course the voice is certainly not entirely anonymous, and there are many cases where the user is easily identified by friends and family who are lis-tening. But there are attempts to make the shows more anonymous by the hosts, who often openly state their preference for using pseudonyms for speak-ers and refraining from using identifying information in stories told about others. These rules are often stated on the websites for the shows, alongside other rules about community norms such as respecting one another or avoid-ing profanity.

The practice of anonymity is particularly important within tightly knit Hmong communities, where all those who share a single last name are consid-ered to be part of one's extended family.[4] Given that participants frequently talk about matters that are deeply personal or could potentially bring shame to themselves and their families, the presumption of anonymity can help to shield participants from negative social consequences. Discussions on the shows often delve into issues of physical, mental, and emotional health; marital issues such as infidelity, polygamy, child brides, divorce, or domestic violence; or the every-day struggles and problems that individuals are facing. Many interview sub-jects described a sense that gossip about these kinds of issues spreads rapidly within the face-to-face communication networks of Hmong extended families, and that any salacious tidbit of information would quickly become known by everyone in their family and local community. In this context, it makes sense that Hmong individuals might seek out a communicative space that is distinctly Hmong, but that is not reliant on family networks. It is the feeling of speak-ing to a diasporic audience—which stands in opposition to conversing with community members from one's own family, city, or geographic region—that draws many participants to the calls.

Beyond creating a sense of security and safety, teleconference radio programs also utilize their ability to transcend regional boundaries to create a platform for discussing issues of global significance. This can include more personal issues, such as seeking to find others who spent time in certain refugee camps, or who are similarly nostalgic about growing up in a village in Laos. But there are also many conversations about the more serious problems facing Hmong families in the United States some forty years after the first refugees began to arrive. For instance, one of the most commonly debated topics discussed on the shows is abusive international marriages, or the practice of Hmong Amer-ican men traveling to Laos, China, or Thailand to find a spouse (Dabby-Chinoy 2012). Many of these marriages become a problem when the bride is underage, does not consent to the partnership, or is subsequently abandoned. Hmong families in the United States are negatively impacted when husbands pressure their first wives for a divorce in order to engage in international marriages, and then the wife and children struggle with poverty, lack of child support, and the negative social stigma attached to divorce in Hmong communities. This extremely complex issue reflects the transnational positioning of Hmong in the diaspora, as it is premised on the idea that Hmong Americans are now adjusting to their increasing power and wealth relative to Hmong in Asia, or are attempting to maintain traditional customs amid shifting contemporary gender roles. Hmong teleconference radio programs thus provide an ideal platform for allowing Hmong voices from across the world to address this issue—including sharing stories about friends and family members who are experiencing this problem, providing advice and support to those who have been affected, and engaging in debates about the meaning of this practice for Hmong culture.

Hmong Women as Owners, Hosts, and Listeners

As discussed in the previous chapters, traditional Hmong media industries are in line with all mainstream media industries in the United States (Federal Communications Commission 2014) in being largely owned and staffed by men. Within this context, it is particularly noteworthy that Hmong teleconference radio programs are largely owned, operated, and hosted by women. As this chapter and the next chapter reveal, the low barriers for entry to micro media entrepreneurship mean that marginalized populations are utilizing this opportunity to own and control their own media industries in ways that may challenge the norm. This gender imbalance is visible on the webpages for radio programs like *Xov Tooj Cua Phooj Ywg Tiam 21*, where there are photo rosters of DJs that consist of an array of dozens of women in traditional and contemporary Hmong clothing. Beyond the information available on websites, I also spoke to many owners who confirmed that the majority of their DJs and hosts were women. One owner stated: "On our show it seems that the men do not have time to become hosts since they seem to have duties that help out with families. So most of the men are spending their time hunting, or having family duties away from the home while leaving the wives home alone. That is why there is a majority of women DJs. We have about 70 percent women and 30 percent men." Beyond owning the shows and serving as DJs, Hmong women are also perceived to be the primary audience of callers and listeners. This is not a quantifiable statistic, as the gender breakdown of those on the conference calls is not collected, but the participants I spoke to believed this to be the case. Moreover, many participants characterized the callers in gendered terms, talking about their wives, sisters, mothers, aunts, and other women they knew who listened to the shows.

Mobile phones are often understood as a domestic technology that blurs the line between the home and the workplace (Lim 2014), and this is clearly the case for women who operate and participate in Hmong teleconference radio programs. Using nothing but their mobile phone, they are able to integrate the labor of owning a conference call number or hosting a show into the rhythms of their everyday life. The participants I spoke to often described negotiating the demands of a day job as well as their familial role as wife, mother, and any number of other extended familial obligations. Yet the gendering of these shows was not a commonly recognized feature of Hmong teleconference radio. While women clearly play an important role in shaping this emergent media industry, it was rare for participants to describe the programs as being by, for, or about women. When asked about whether or not the prevalence of women hosts had an impact on the shows or their function, listeners were often ambivalent and indicated this was something they had not thought about before. We can see this kind of thinking in the following statement from a college-aged female listener: "Both women and men are on there. I would say there are more women hosting. But there are also men. The issues that I heard are mostly related to women's issues, like there will be the issue of how married men might try to go to Laos and marry a younger woman, and they talk about if they should do that or if it's wrong of them to do it. So in a way, mostly women's issues. Men don't have a lot of issues going on, since in the Hmong culture the men have more rights." We can see that her initial response was to back away from the claim that the shows were dominated by women, but that she slowly began to discuss how this was so. By the end of her statement, she connected the kinds of topics being discussed to what she saw as the patriarchal nature of Hmong culture and the practice of Hmong men marrying younger women from Laos— topics that frequently arose in conversations about Hmong culture, particularly among college-aged participants. It was often taken for granted by female participants that Hmong culture had a conservative perspective on gender roles and that young Hmong women faced difficulty in gaining social power. One second-generation female listener stated, "Growing up as a Hmong girl, you are taught to be submissive and silent and you couldn't really speak out. You had to be obedient. Throughout my life that's how I was taught. If I ever spoke out, I was treated as the girl who would not get a suitable husband." We can see strong evidence of patriarchal norms in this statement, in everything from the silencing of girls and women to the heteronormative expectation that girls and women must prepare their whole lives for marriage to a man.[5] These norms influenced the way that the shows were perceived in relation to gender, as it was assumed that the status quo for Hmong culture was to center patriarchy and the voices of men.

One of the unique ways that the culturally specific, participatory format of Hmong teleconference radio was deployed by women was to create a form of literacy education. I visited a woman named Plia at home in her apartment, which she shared with her sons. She began the interview by telling me that she had a limited educational background. Currently in her fifties, she had come to the United States over twenty-five years earlier and tried to learn English, but struggled and gave up. She stated, "I know how to write my address and my name, nothing more than that." We proceeded to discuss all of the different forms of media that she commonly paid attention to, including her cell phone. She affirmed that she did like to listen to storytelling through the teleconference radio programs, as well as news reports. Yet my ears perked up when she said that she also used the phone for a class that was held four days a week on the topic of Hmong literacy. Specifically, Plia had been learning the Hmong script called *pahawh*, an indigenous form of writing that is attributed to a messianic movement that arose in the 1950s. When I expressed confusion about how she might be learning to read and write script from the audio format of the teleconference, she ran to another room to retrieve a workbook. She flipped through the photocopied and laminated pages and explained that she and the other students followed along in the workbook while the teacher read the text. Plia spoke about the lessons as though she only participated in them to pass the time in the evening, but their importance in providing an educational opportunity was clear.

Many other participants directly connected these kinds of lessons and conversations to their liberatory potential for Hmong women. One woman in her forties stated that she thought listening to the conference calls was positive for Hmong people because in a society that often devalues women's opinions, the radio programs could go so far as to support women who may be suicidal. She said: "In this culture there's a lot of suicide for women because they hold things to themselves. I've heard a woman say, if I didn't come to this conference call, I would have commit suicide two years ago. But someone told me to listen and I realized I'm not the only one who faced this issue, someone has the same problems as I do." Another young woman said that some men did not want to let their wives listen to the shows because they might get ideas about how to stand up for themselves. These stories offer strong examples of the way that teleconference radio programs could play a transformative role in the lives of their female participants, opening up communication networks for validation and support during difficult times.

Women's Taboo Conversations

Beyond giving women a space to voice their perspectives and hear responses to their problems, the shows also provided a rare opportunity for women to voice their perspective on sensitive or intimate topics. For instance, during interviews many participants talked about the fact that romantic relationships were often discussed within Hmong teleconference radio programs. This included everything from advice about how to improve one's relationship to explicit discussions about sex, marital infidelity, domestic abuse, child brides, polygamy, and other taboo subjects. One female DJ from Wisconsin stated that these were among the most popular issues: "Even though people say topics are taboo, those are the ones that have the highest numbers [of listeners]. We are lying to ourselves or we're still hiding in the closet but yet we want to listen. For example, people don't like to talk about behaviors like sex behaviors or romantic stuff. Hmong people think it's taboo to talk about love between men and women. But they listen all day and night when it comes to those topics that attract the most callers. So I'm saying they say one thing and do another." This description points to a reason for the popularity of these shows—they often discuss topics that people feel uncomfortable talking about, or are unable to talk about, among their close friends and family. On the shows, women are able to share stories, get advice, hear about people who are in similar difficult situations, and discuss important issues that would otherwise be considered taboo and silenced.

While all cultures have issues that are considered taboo, Hmong culture in particular can be very guarded around issues of sexuality. In a study about family secrets, researchers found that a high percentage of Hmong families thought that marital arguments, extramarital affairs, marital violence and abuse, delinquent children, and personal issues such as depression and financial problems should not be talked about outside of the nuclear family (Xiong et al. 2006). This is significant because the fear of stigma and shame can make Hmong women less likely to seek professional help or utilize services for these kinds of issues, despite their significance in maintaining healthy families. Hmong girls have also been found to encounter extreme challenges in communicating with their parents about sexual health issues due to a combination of factors, including proscriptions within the Hmong community against open conversations about sex and sexuality (Meschke and Dettmer 2012). If this is the case, then we can see Hmong teleconference radio as an important intervention in this dearth of information and suppression of discourse surrounding these issues.

Given the focus on anonymity and the dispersed geographic reach of the shows, these shows contribute to a sense that one's own family members are not listening in. Yet the closed nature of the shows being conducted only in Hmong language also allows a degree of cultural specificity that helps participants to feel understood and validated as members of an often marginalized ethnic community. This feeling of intimacy that comes from participating in the mobile public constituted within Hmong teleconference radio programs reflects Hjorth and Lim's (2012) theorization of mobile intimacies. They argue that women are most implicated in the turn to mobile media practices for the blending of work and leisure, private and public—both of which can be seen in the way that women facilitate conversations about extremely personal subjects on a conference call that is open to hundreds of listeners. Rather than discussing current affairs or public events, the most common topics of discussion are simply the personal stories and inquiries that participants want to share with others who are like them. One elderly female listener spoke about the shows that she felt were the most popular and beneficial: "During the times and topics that are being discussed about how to keep your husband from not having a girlfriend or if he does have one, what can you do to bring him back, love him and your family back so that it does not end up being destroyed, and what can you do to help it. It is topics like this that brings out a lot of listeners and speakers to the shows." These discussions are of course no replacement for professional counseling, sex education, or other kinds of meaningful conversation with trusted family members that many Hmong women seek. Nevertheless, we can see that this form of micro media is opening up new pathways for women's communication that reside outside of the cultural boundaries and limitations that traditionally serve to silence conversation on a number of important subjects.

Belittling Women's Labor and Participation in Media

While the opportunities provided to women by Hmong teleconference radio are encouraging, it is important to temper this optimistic reading by considering some of the ways that its impact might be limited. First, some women who regularly participated in the shows believed that the women who owned or hosted the teleconference programs were not necessarily progressively minded, but could in fact be very traditional and conservative. I spoke to one woman who was a university professor and served as a cohost for a show with a male colleague who had invited her to help facilitate conversations about education. Yet she increasingly grew frustrated with what she considered to be "ultraconservative" views condemning interracial relationships and same-sex marriage. In addition, she hypothesized that the shows might draw participants with these beliefs because hosting the shows demanded extremely proficient Hmong language skills. She stated, "The people who tend to speak Hmong very well aren't as acculturated, they're first generation who haven't adopted Western views. And also it's not a good idea for someone who's not traditional to lead those shows because they might get eaten alive." This perspective seems to imply that the programs did not always provide a space for challenging hegemonic norms or giving voice to oppressed viewpoints. We can also note from these statements that the nature of the show's reliance on the oral tradition can be a strength when it allows participants to voice controversial opinions under the cloak of visual anonymity, but that the language skills and fluency of participants become so central that it may exclude participants who are less confident about their Hmong speaking skills.

Beyond political restrictions within the content itself, the shows are also limited by the fact that they are often perceived in negative ways. The general response to the existence and development of teleconference radio among the Hmong Americans I interviewed ranged from mildly positive or neutral to outright condemnation and disapproval. Negative perceptions of the programs predominated, with very few participants expressing strong support or enthusiasm for this form of communication. As might be expected, the strongest voices of criticism came from interviews with the entrepreneur-owners who participated in more traditional Hmong broadcast media, such as radio and television. This makes sense because the teleconference shows could be perceived as competition to their own programming. Their disdain for the shows became evident in numerous criticisms—including that the sound of the shows was inferior because it was not clear and had a lot of static, that the DJs could not properly control their audience and allowed everyone to talk at once, and that they were merely "wannabe" news shows.

The most common and forceful complaint about the shows was that they were not regulated in the same way as "real" radio stations, which meant that they could talk in ways that are indecent, profane, or taboo. This includes discussions of topics such as sex and religion, which traditional broadcasters felt they were restricted from discussing. Worst of all was the fact that on Hmong teleconference radio programs, people did not have to tell the truth, and thus the programs often participated in spreading poorly researched misinformation. Many traditional radio broadcasters interviewed for this study worried about the quality of information that was being spread using the teleconference radio programs because it was the professional responsibility of broadcasters like themselves to conduct research, vet their facts, and only invite credentialed experts to speak about serious issues on their programs. Teleconference radio programs were likened to "online chatrooms" instead of journalism, and many people could cite health or public safety stories they were being spread through the teleconference programs that were dangerously incorrect.

The fact that many of these critiques come from Hmong American media entrepreneurs whom we have seen relying on the development of a media empire comprised of multiple outlets might seem strange because they are clearly not opposed to diversifying their own formats. In order to understand what makes Hmong teleconference programs different from more traditional outlets, we must recognize that these value-laden critiques reflect the same cultural hierarchies that all female-centered media face. Women who participate in Hmong teleconference radio are criticized for engaging in discourse that relies on an overabundance of emotion and is lacking in rational or intellectual contributions to society. The gendering of media technologies and programming is often connected to assumptions that men's ways of thinking—and thus the media that they produce and consume—are thought to be rational and intellectual, while women's media are thought to be more emotional, affectively volatile, and melodramatic. These critiques can also be understood within the context of how women were historically treated within radio industries, as women have historically been considered inferior radio announcers. Michele Hilmes (1997) cites an outpouring of misogynistic rhetoric that surrounded the advent of female announcers, including questions about whether women's voices and vocal performances could possibly compare to the authority, affective modulation, volume, personality, appeal, experience, or expertise of men. Although women nevertheless made headway into the radio arena, such criticisms of women's voices continue to this day, with women being policed for upspeak and vocal fry, among other maligned aural qualities (Tiffe and Hoffman 2017).

Together, these criticisms serve to wholly obscure the actual labor of the women who put many long hours into creating and running these programs. We can acknowledge that being seen as a competitor or threat to traditional media professionals is actually a sign of their legitimacy, but in my conversations with Hmong Americans it is clear that the belittling and dismissal of the women who run these programs has effectively diminished their status as communication and media leaders. While traditional broadcast professionals are often recognized by community organizations or made visible at cultural events, the women who run these programs are never given the same treatment. As with so many women who labor invisibly to provide a platform for women's voices, Hmong teleconference radio owners are given little tangible reward for their efforts.

Pathologizing and Feminizing Listeners

Criticisms of Hmong teleconference radio also extended beyond the perspectives of traditional broadcasters, with many other Hmong community members expressing strong concern or disdain for the shows. Sometimes these feelings manifested in subtle ways, such as participants laughing nervously when they talked about how often someone they knew called into the shows. Most participants knew someone who called into the shows every day and left the phone on all day long. This sense that regular participants were "always on the phone" was sometimes pathologized as an "addiction" to the shows, which was seen as sad or strange. One woman recalled that her mother listened to the show so excessively that the phone company canceled her phone contract. Others more explicitly discussed the negative social impact of the shows, such as this comment: "A lady called me and said, my husband is listening to [the mobile phone shows] day and night! Even after they cook he doesn't want to eat anymore, he keeps listening to that radio! It creates probably marriage disturbance, you know? Misunderstandings, something like that." There was often a perception that listening to the shows could become an impediment to many forms of health, including physical, mental, emotional, and spiritual wellness. It became clear that calling into the shows was seen as a time-wasting activity that indicated a lower status in society, or at least simply that this was an activity that many participants found shameful or less desirable.

These sentiments that the shows had a negative social impact or a lesser social status must again be connected to the assumption that participants were women, or that they inhabited a panoply of feminized or socially inferior positions. One man described his perception of the audience in terms of both gender and status: "I was told a lot of people who are listening are distressed people like widows or people with spiritual problems, all those people who have time to listen to it. A working person doesn't have time, but a lot of people listen to it. There's no way to tell who listens, but probably more women." Another person stated that the conference was good for people who had disabilities or were older than sixty, since neither could work anymore and this was a way for them to connect to other adults. Such comments reveal a common perception that Hmong teleconference radio is primarily the purview of women and other individuals with less social capital in Hmong society. These assumptions align with the way that Kylie Jarrett (2014) finds that "the free, unpaid, affective, immaterial labor of the digital economy" suffers the same lowly status as "women's work" within contemporary capitalism, as neither are attributed an appropriate use value (14). In the case of Hmong teleconference radio, the devalued designation of "women's work" is overdetermined through assumptions about what type of people participate in the programs, what type of conversations take place, and what contributions these programs make to Hmong culture more generally.

This understanding of the audience for Hmong teleconference radio can also be connected to discourses of mobility, as the experiences of Hmong refugees being dispersed from their home country and arriving in the United States are marked by both mobilities and immobilities. In one sense, many Hmong in the diaspora are transnational migrants who have connections to other Hmong all over the world, which is what necessitates the creation of this global form of communication. Yet these experiences are often coupled with the immobility of being unable to work in the United States due to mental and physical health problems, as well as a lack of language skills or literacy (Collier, Munger, and Moua 2012). One woman described why her mother listens to teleconference radio programs: "Because of language barriers she can't listen to American radio, she can't listen to what's going on. Because of mobility issues she can't drive or walk around the neighborhood very much. She needs to know what's going on in the world, but she can't listen to American news. So she listens to [mobile phone shows] to keep her entertained." Thus it is important to acknowledge the complicated interplay between the opportunities afforded by mobile phones and the social circumstances that necessitate their usage and integration into daily life. Unlike many Asian immigrant populations in the United States, many Hmong Americans do not have reliable internet connections or the technical literacy for using their computer or a smartphone to access any other forms of global media. Teleconference radio programs then become a necessary lifeline to the outside world because so many other opportunities for communication, social interaction, or information gathering are unavailable.

Fears of Unregulated Debates

Other concerns about the shows were that they were harmful to Hmong society because they provided an outlet for so much fighting, disagreement, and expression of negative emotions. In yet another gendered form of critique, the Hmong women on the shows were often criticized for not having appropriately gentle voices, or for speaking too harshly and engaging in arguments. Such complaints extended to the entire premise of the programs, as interview subjects stated that callers and hosts who engaged in impassioned debate on topics of central importance to Hmong society were seen as failing to fulfill the mission of radio programming. One man said: "I get that arguing is part of a debate or a discussion, but most of the time their arguments are pretty elementary. They resort to a lot of name-calling. I talked to my dad yesterday and he said you shouldn't listen to them because they don't do anything productive. Radio is supposed to bring people together, and these type of shows that are primarily arguments don't do that. That's why I don't like them." When combined with the perception that the shows also focused on taboo topics such as sexuality and transgressive behaviors, many worried that the shows were giving Hmong communities around the world a bad impression of Hmong Americans. There was a perception that Hmong Americans did most of the talking, but that listeners were from all over the world, tuning into learn about Hmong American life and culture. When the topics of the shows revolved around Hmong Americans cheating on their spouses, getting divorces, wanting to marry members of their own clan, moving to Laos to marry a child bride, engaging in polygamy, or other shameful behaviors, this was feared to give Hmong Americans a bad reputation.

The fear of allowing an outlet for unregulated discourse and debate seems to ignore the ways in which these characteristics can be seen as a strength, as well as the way that the shows have evolved over the years. One DJ I spoke to agreed that the shows were very chaotic when they first opened the lines and invited callers to participate in 2009. People would talk on top of one another and rogue participants could use the open airway to say whatever they wanted. Yet over time, DJs and callers together created and enforced a set of community agreements that served to regulate the space while still allowing everyone to have their say. Although there can still be interruptions, participants became quite respectful in deciding when to speak up, often allowing the host to assign numbers to participants and then waiting to be called on—a remarkable feat of turn taking for a collective conversation that can include thousands of participants. The polyvocality of the teleconference radio programs could easily result in overwhelming cacophony or sonic pandemonium if even a small number of participants refused to participate in listening as much as they did in speaking up. But the reality is that teleconference radio programs are often indistinguishable from traditional radio programs to their listeners because participants respect the explicit or implicit contract of participation. The agreed-upon values of listening and giving equal access to speakers is what leads to the creation of a lively counter-public sphere for members of the Hmong diaspora to come together and discuss important issues outside of the mainstream media—where Hmong voices and Hmong women's voices, as well as other Asian American immigrant voices, are systemically silenced.

The existence of this public forum for debate offers the ability to facilitate discourse about issues that strike to the very core of what it means to be Hmong—how to uphold cultural practices and norms, how to negotiate cultural change, how to integrate or resist assimilation into American society, or how to be successful in a challenging world. Indeed, the very concept of a democratic and productive public sphere is often argued to rest on the ability of individuals to express themselves openly, engaging in debates and arguments that are unregulated and unruly (Connery 1997). Zizi Papacharissi (2004) argues that in assessing the democratic potential for a communicative space, we must be careful not to demand mere politeness as a marker of healthy interaction, as "a sharply-defined conceptual distinction between civility and politeness acknowledges the passion, unpredictability, and robustness of human nature and conversation, with the understanding that democracy can merit a heated discussion" (262).

These programs are also inherently multidirectional, allowing individuals throughout the Hmong diaspora to listen, speak, or take on a leadership role regardless of their geographic location. There does not seem to be an inherent power structure within the geographic reach of the shows that privileges a one-way flow from Laos, Thailand, Vietnam, the United States, or other specific spaces within the Hmong diaspora. Rather, this invitation for diverse and conflicting perspectives reflects a community in motion, struggling against the hegemonic and patriarchal voices that continually participate in silencing some voices and elevating others. Frequent discussions about what it means to be Hmong and how best to maintain Hmong culture work to continually constitute and reconstitute Hmong identity through these shows. DJs and callers hold forth on these topics on a daily basis, providing listeners with a wide breadth of perspectives on the meaning of Hmong identities in today's society. As a people who are dispersed across the globe and have no territorial homeland, diasporic Hmong are continually faced with the threat of losing their own unique culture and identity to the processes of assimilation and acculturation.

In providing a forum for explicit discussion about what it means to be Hmong in a site that is marked by disharmony and a multiplicity of voices, this emerging and constantly evolving form of media allows opportunities for growth and change, rather than settling on a single rendering of Hmong life in the diaspora.

Conclusion: Gendered Participation and Its Limits

This investigation of Hmong teleconference radio reveals the potential for micro media to facilitate interaction and participation with some of the most vulnerable members of a community. Here we see the active role that some Hmong American women are playing in using mobile media to spread information and facilitate dialogue. In creating their own form of media industry, they are able to make use of new technologies in a way that strengthens communication within portions of the Hmong diaspora through the format's openness, accessibility, and participatory nature—reminding us that "women's work" can include the creation of global platforms poised to powerfully impact the shape of a diasporic culture. Yet in exploring the gendered discourses that surround this form of Hmong media culture and the use of the phone, we are also reminded that the existence of a mobile platform that facilitates women's participation does not automatically challenge the patriarchal status quo. The opportunities for counterhegemony provided by these programs are not always recognized or validated, and those who create and use them are often left invisible and marginalized.

As new media technologies continue to develop and open up new opportunities for grassroots forms of global communication, we must be attendant to the way they might facilitate the creation of innovative micro media outlets—but also to the gendered dynamics of participation and the way that such communication is valued. This research suggests that there are likely other forms of mobile communication being developed within other communities who struggle against some of the same constraints, and whose emerging forms of media may similarly intersect with gender and gendered discourses. Hmong teleconference radio programs show us one way that more traditional media industries of film, television, and online platforms can be bypassed in order to create and participate in a less professional forum for sharing stories and hosting debates. It is within these messy, open-ended, everyday conversations that we must continue to ask whose voices are invited to participate and what is accomplished when they are allowed to do so.

5

Queer Sounds

●●●●●●●●●●●●●●●●●●●●●●●●

Podcasting and
Audio Archives

At a summit for youth of color in Wisconsin, a twenty-year-old Hmong trans activist named Kaleb presented a keynote titled "There Is No Word in My Language to Describe My Sexual Orientation, Therefore I Do Not Exist." The speech explored the struggles that Kaleb had endured as a child who felt uncomfortable fitting into the gendered expectations for Hmong girls, and the pain of having parents who responded with detachment and isolation rather than understanding. While all queer and gender nonconforming youth face struggles in coming to terms with identities that challenge social norms, Kaleb's speech additionally highlighted the difficulties faced by queer Hmong individuals in even finding the language to describe their identities. Some queer individuals use English words such as lesbian, gay, trans, or queer to describe themselves. Others have invented new terms in the Hmong language to describe gender nonconforming identities, such as the use of the term *tub-ntxhais* as a blend of terms for son (*tub*) and daughter (*ntxhais*).

The creation of Hmong media outlets featuring the voices of queer Hmong individuals provides an important intervention in supporting those who are facing these particular struggles. Not only do queer media provide the opportunity for developing a more extensive discourse and vocabulary for talking about queer Hmong issues, but they also serve as a platform for highlighting and empowering members of the community who are out and proud. This chapter explores three forms of audio media that are intended to participate in queering Hmong America—a radio show called *Nplooj*, a podcast called *Hoochim*, and a radio series called *Poj Laib / Bad Hmong Girl*. Each of these programs reflects the possibility for micro media industries to enable small, marginalized populations to represent themselves—both to others within their community and to outsiders.

While the previous chapter discussed the salience of audio media in the Hmong diaspora, the teleconference radio programs discussed there are largely made by and for first-generation or 1.5-generation Hmong Americans (that is, those who were born abroad and immigrated as adults, or those who were born abroad and immigrated as children). This includes Hmong elders, but also younger adults who are part of more recent waves of immigration and thus do not speak fluent English. The general sense that "Hmong radio" is mostly consumed by older generations is prevalent; many of the Hmong American college students I have spoken with have little interest in the broader category of Hmong media, and their only exposure to Hmong media is through their parents and grandparents. But the three queer programs examined in this chapter provide an example of the kind of culturally specific audio media that Hmong millennials are producing and consuming. It reveals the reality that not all Hmong youth have assimilated into the habit of only engaging with mainstream American media and left ethnic media to the elderly immigrant population; on the contrary, there are clearly Hmong youth and young adults who are invested in creating media by and for their generation. When these texts are in English, it is also possible that non-Hmong audiences can encounter and learn from them as well.

This chapter begins with a discussion of Hmong sexuality and sexual orientation before investigating three different forms of queer aural media through interviews with producers and analysis of their programs. These queer Hmong micro media platforms are an important site for analysis because their explicit position of marginality can help us to better reflect on the accepted norms of the larger ecology of Hmong media. While all micro media industries emerge from a position of relative marginality due to resource scarcity and other limits, we can nonetheless identify a kind of hegemonic discourse that settles across the individual contributions to Hmong American media ecologies—one that centers normative gender roles and heterosexuality. Conversations with the creators of queer Hmong media programs help us to understand the complex dynamics inherent to a micro media ecology—including the fact that essentializing narratives that promote a singular understanding of a community can become normalized and upheld, but also that there is possibility for these narratives to be disrupted and renegotiated.

Since the forms of queer media studied here are audio, it also helps us consider the innovations that Hmong micro media entrepreneurs make in order to overcome the challenges faced in terms of archiving their content for future listeners. Radio and other audio performances are so often ephemeral or only accessible live, which might dampen the political impact of these counterhegemonic programs. Hmong radio in particular has rarely been included in any radio archiving projects, and it is difficult to locate any systematic or institutionalized documentation of most forms of Hmong aural media (Lopez 2018). Each of the queer audio programs investigated here strategically augment the longevity of their programs as a way of increasing the reach and influence of their political interventions. These findings reveal the significance of specific technological affordances in shaping how micro media industries and their participants can both reify and challenge dominant cultural norms.

Hmong American LGBTQ+ Experiences

The field of queer and LGBTQ+ Hmong studies has been slow to develop, as has been the case with scholarship on queer Asian Americans more broadly (Eng and Hom 1998). But since the late 2000s, there have been a number of researchers dedicated to better understanding the specific experiences of Hmong American lesbian, gay, bisexual, trans, and queer individuals. Some of this work has come from fields such as social work and psychology, with the intention of helping clinicians and service providers better develop more nuanced interventions for those with "multiple and conflicting identities" (Boulden 2009, 135). The process of coming out as LGBTQ+ is often assumed to be a necessary step toward embracing one's true self, but for Asian Americans and Hmong Americans specifically there are often complex cultural factors that make it difficult to reveal their nonnormative gender or sexuality to their immigrant-generation parents. For Hmong Americans, these include a lack of Hmong language and terminology for LGBTQ+ identities, a focus on heteronormative kinship relations for identifying one's place within the community, and a host of cultural customs and religious ceremonies that rely on static conceptions of gender. As a result, many Hmong LGBTQ+ people face threats ranging from anxiety and depression to social ostracization and violence.

Much of the research on Hmong sexuality has focused on gay men, with Bruce Thao (2016) claiming that "we must move beyond a gaze fixed on gay Hmong men as the quintessential representation of all that is queer and Hmong" (299). Scholars have criticized this limited focus for the way that it reifies problematic binaries around culture and sexuality. This includes assumptions that the only options for responding to LGBTQ+ people are celebration or rejection, and the attendant assumption that Hmong culture itself is necessarily inhospitable to LGBTQ+ identities. Kong Pheng Pha (2016) connects this to the way that Americans often characterize Hmong culture as hyperheterosexual through emphasizing practices such as bride kidnapping, bride price, child brides, polygamy, and having lots of children. Because each of these deviant sexual practices is undeniably heterosexual, the focus on them serves to indelibly link Hmong culture with heterosexuality. As a by-product of this ideological process, queer Hmong identities are then obscured and made to seem as if they do not exist. But the reality is that Hmong culture (as with all ethnic cultures) is dynamic and complex, and there are multiple ways in which Hmong Americans are continually negotiating their sexualities and gender identities through and within Hmong culture. Pha (2016) states that "Hmong queers cannot simply contemplate sadness every single day of their lives" (304) and strives to explore the ways in which he and other Hmong Americans demonstrate agency in seeking out queer Hmong joy. Bic Ngo has produced a number of studies on Hmong sexuality, and she similarly emphasizes the way that Hmong culture is not static, arguing that rigid narratives of rejecting or accepting LGBTQ+ identities can be broken down in complex ways within a single person, or a single family over time (Ngo 2012a; Ngo 2012b; Ngo and Kwon 2015).

Bruce Thao (2016) models this dynamic in his deep dive into the data reported in the Queer Southeast Asian Census, a participatory survey project that was the first of its kind to gather data on LGBTQ+ Southeast Asian Americans. First, he discusses the way that queer Hmong couplings complicate traditional customs around Hmong marriage, family and kinship structures, naming, and understandings of lineage. This includes fears around reproduction because "particularly for a community that has experienced centuries of persecution, war, migration, and statelessness, the . . . fear of extinction is not a far-fetched idea" (282). Yet he also finds that Hmong LGBTQ+ "embrace their families, value Hmong culture, and seek to be loved and accepted for who they are . . . through the negotiation of these identities and multiple spaces, they find agency and power" (283). One of the ways that we have seen this taking place is through the formation of a number of queer Hmong organizations. The earliest of these was Shades of Yellow (SOY), which was started in 2003 as a social space for Hmong LGBTQ+ Minnesotans to meet up and support one another. SOY's members hosted open mics and storytelling events, support groups, parties and celebrations, and an annual Hmong New Year event. Another organization that provides a space for queer Hmong is Freedom, Inc. in Madison, Wisconsin. Although they are a diverse organization serving Black, Hmong, and Khmer communities, their model of leadership has always centered queer development and they have culturally specific programming that focuses on Southeast Asian women, gender nonconforming people, and queer folks.

There are also many individual activists who have worked hard to support the queer Hmong community. One such individual is Linda Her, who served as the executive director of the Asian American Organizing Project and an organizer with Trust Project MN, and spearheaded the development of a collective called MidWest Solidarity Movement (MWSM). One of the projects of MWSM was to collect and publish a series of Hmong LGBTQQI Coming OUT stories on their blog. The thirty-four stories were published as blog entries at the MidWest Solidarity Movement website (mwsmovement.com), and together comprise a larger data set than any academic study that had been conducted on the topic of being queer and Hmong. Her is also one of the four hosts for the podcast *Hoochim*, which is one of the audio programs I closely examine in order to consider its disruptive potential within Hmong media ecologies.

This media content is an important addition to the kind of support offered by family networks, organizations, and individuals. Bic Ngo (2012b) argues that there is indeed potential for mediated networks to help provide the kinds of "social, political, and economic support systems that contribute to the spiritual, emotional, and physical well-being of Hmong Americans" (129). Another example of this can be seen in the work of Freedom, Inc. to produce a media campaign in 2013 called "Love is Love." The campaign centered on a series of images that depicted queer Black and Hmong people who were happy, healthy, and respected members of their community. Through hanging posters with the images in their local communities, sending postcards printed with the messages to their members, and spreading the digital images through their online social media platforms, they sought to increase awareness and acceptance of queer Black and Hmong people (Lopez 2015). In 2015, their youth members created a series of YouTube videos that further explored the messages of the videos through interviews with queer Black and Hmong leaders in the organization. This chapter builds from these insights on the needs of LGBTQ+ Hmong Americans by expanding the category of Hmong LGBTQ+ media to include podcasting and community radio—two forms of audio micro media that Hmong American women and queer folks are using to grow their reach and influence.

Podcasting as Micro Media Industry

The term "podcast" refers to a compressed audio file that allows for time-shifted listening practices, in contrast to the liveness of radio broadcasts. Podcasting practices have been celebrated because the accessibility of production opened up the category of radio broadcasting to everyday users who could now produce their own content. As mentioned in earlier chapters, the financial resources necessary for owning, operating, and staffing a radio station are significant, as well as dependent on being able to acquire a license to broadcast from the FCC. Although podcasting demands some technological literacy, podcasts are generally free to create and distribute through publishing to a plethora of available podcast directories, including Apple's iTunes, Stitcher, and SoundCloud.

These democratizing conditions blur the lines between podcasts as professional media and user-generated content.

The popularity of the format has led to the rise of a number of well-funded, well-staffed podcasting corporations. For instance, Gimlet Media is a podcasting network that in 2017 had over eighty staff members and was valued at $70 million (Gimlet Media 2017; Kafka 2017). In 2018, the podcasting network Radiotopia had seventeen different shows that were downloaded over 18 million times per month (Taylor 2018), and the most popular podcasts across the board were produced by the podcasting arm of traditional media outlets such as NPR, the Public Radio Exchange (PRX), the *New York Times*, and ESPN. Alongside the rise of professionalized content such as this, there has been a corresponding development of elevated expectations for podcast quality, such as sharper sound, more complex editing, and the use of music and sound effects. There has also been an increase in the monetization of podcasts, where it has become commonplace for podcasts to include advertising that straightforwardly demarcates financial support.

Despite these shifts, podcasting still provides an opportunity for amateurs and everyday media consumers to get involved in producing this form of media for niche audiences. Markman and Sawyer (2014) describe podcasting as a marketplace with a long tail (Anderson 2006), meaning that the handful of popular and professionally produced podcasts are actually in the minority. The majority of the podcasting marketplace is taken up by independent producers who are not podcasting full time and only reach small audiences. This long tail of podcasting is composed of entities that fall within the category of micro media industry. Most podcasting teams consist of a host and a producer, and sometimes an audio engineer as well, but these teams are clearly operating on the microscale. This is particularly true for Asian American podcasters, few of whom have the financial resources or media access to hire producers, editors, or other staff. Within the eleven Asian American podcasts included in the network called Potluck Podcast Collective in 2019, all fell under the category of micro media industry with their host or hosts taking on every aspect of production.

As of 2019, podcasting had not become very widespread as a form of Hmong media. Although a handful of Hmong radio stations started to rebroadcast some of their programs as podcasts, there were very few podcasts that specifically focus on Hmong content. A religious podcast called *Yexus Communitas* focusing on Hmong Americans and Christianity broadcast a number of episodes in early 2018. An organization called Hmong Innovating Politics also briefly hosted a show called *Southeast Asian American Podcast Network* that featured interviews with Hmong American activists. Beyond these few episodes, there were few other Hmong-led podcasts, which made the female-led

Hoochim podcast even more significant. In this examination of a media format that is already heavily populated with micro media entrepreneurs, we can see the possibility for those who are doubly marginalized to participate—while also using their platform to challenge previous norms and exclusions.

Hoochim Podcast

The first episode of the *Hoochim* podcast was recorded on July 10, 2015, and posted days later. Each show begins with a brief introduction from each of the participants against the backdrop of a softly played *qeej*, a traditional Hmong reed instrument. Then comes the show's exuberantly voiced tagline: "We're four Hmong girls talking about things that matter such as . . . everything!" In the first episode, the hosts jump into a discussion of a recent incident at a Hmong soccer tournament in St. Paul. There was controversy over accusations that an organization was exploiting the opportunity for financial profit by banning athletes from bringing their own water and then overpricing the water bottles sold inside the tournament. It begins as a discussion about the unfair cost of bottled water, but quickly becomes a complex conversation about the political framing of the event in relation to Hmong identity. Participants raise questions about celebrating the famed Hmong leader General Vang Pao on the American Fourth of July holiday, racial inclusion for St. Paul's refugee populations, the meaning of "freedom" for Hmong people, the relationship between Hmong consumer dollars and the city of St. Paul, and other issues. This is the hallmark of their show—mixing humor, personal storytelling, discussions of local issues, and pontification on broader political concerns. In their first two years, they posted a total of fourteen episodes before starting to slow down and post more infrequently.

The four members of *Hoochim* are Mee Xiong (also spelled Mim Xyooj, using the Hmong Romanized Popular Alphabet), Sandy Oh, Pao Houa Her (Paj Huab Hawj), and Linda Her (Linda Hawj, who was discussed earlier as a queer Hmong American community organizer). Although none had any previous experience in podcasting, they were fans of other podcasts and felt that the medium was a good fit for their project. They liked the fact that podcasting allowed them produce a program without needing to be physically present together, since three of their members lived in St. Paul and one in New England. Two members attended a feminist science fiction convention called WisCon and met the podcasters from *Nerdgasm*, a podcast about gaming and geek culture hosted by two white men. They were encouraged by the hosts of *Nerdgasm* to try making their own podcast, so they decided to go for it. They purchased a microphone, taught themselves how to mix sound using the free software Audacity, and launched *Hoochim*.

The name of the podcast is a mixture of the Hmong word *hwm chim*, which means prestige or authority and is usually used for men, and the English word *hoochie*, which describes provocative women. I interviewed two members in 2018, and they described their goals in a number of different registers. At a basic level, they simply wanted to broadcast the conversations of four Hmong American women about the everyday things that mattered to them. They recognized that their perspectives were often missing from the Hmong media landscape, which was dominated by Hmong men who they felt upheld essentializing narratives about Hmong people. But at a deeper level, they also sought to provide their listeners with tools for disrupting these common narratives through being able to hear a more critical perspective that incorporates intersectional analyses of race, gender, class, and sexuality. They are careful not to claim that their critical thinking comes from being more educated, but because they actively seek to expand beyond a single Hmong narrative.

Hoochim's members are clear about who they intend to reach with their show—they are speaking to Hmong Americans who are comfortable speaking English or Hmonglish (a blend of Hmong and English), and have access to digital technologies like smartphones and the internet. Despite the fact that their podcast is available to a wide audience due to its distribution on mainstream podcast platforms, they do not evince any interest in reaching non-Hmong audiences. The decision about who they want to target has been important for them to identify, because much of the criticism they have received for the show is from those who think it is too limited in reach. Some listeners have complained that their use of English means that it is not for elderly Hmong. But they remain firm in their decisions, arguing that their goal is not to convince elderly populations through the podcast, but to empower young Hmong Americans to have more difficult conversations within their own families and develop their own skills for challenging Hmong norms.

This resistant framing is also embodied by their hosts, particularly in the way they are described on the *Hoochim* website's "Hosts" page. On it, Pao Houa Her, an artist with an MFA from Yale in photography, provides digitally painted images of each host alongside a paragraph description (figure 1). Mee Xiong, Sandy Oh, and Linda Her are depicted wearing casual clothing and engaging with natural foliage, including a large tree trunk, an array of leaves that obscure Xiong's face, and a potted plant spilling over with blossoms. Pao Houa Her depicts herself nude, lounging among an array of furniture with her breasts exposed, her eyes defiantly staring down the viewer. Her expression, combined with her nudity, communicate confidence and freedom from social constraints. She is fearless about exposing herself and dares the audience to try and challenge her. While Linda Her is clothed in the image, her biography describes her identity as a second-generation Hmong American queer-feminist, artist,

FIG. 1 The website for the *Hoochim* podcast features artistic renderings of its four hosts. Credit: Pao Houa Her.

activist, and community organizer. She also describes her values and goals in relation to her Hmong LGBTQ+ identity:

> At one point in her life, late 1990s to early 2000s, she thought she was the only Hmong gay girl in the world because she was told "there was no Hmong gay person ever," and the US gay and lesbian representation and movement was too White and racist, still is. So if "there was no Hmong gay person ever," and the US gay movement is racist, misogynist, and classist . . . she will boldly step forth to fight for human dignity, where the erasure of many like her before her have lived, but have been violently silenced or murdered.

While the show does not explicitly set out to discuss sexual orientation in the Hmong community, Her clearly voices a queer perspective and issues of sexuality do frequently emerge. They also occasionally bring queer guests onto the show, such as Kong Pheng Pha, a queer scholar and historian, and Chong Vang, a cofounder of Linda Her's MidWest Solidarity Movement.

The aural decisions made by *Hoochim*'s creators also illustrate how they pose a challenge to hegemonic Hmong mediascapes. As Todd Gitlin (1979) argued in his exploration of entertainment television, hegemonic ideologies are deeply rooted in the standardization and routinization of media forms. Formal conventions such as television scheduling, the regularity of commercial breaks, editing techniques, the use of expected settings and character types, and familiar plot resolutions all serve to affirm an ideological status quo. In considering the medium of the podcast, we can also see how decisions to fit within or resist accepted aural norms can have different ideological consequences. For instance, there are some ways in which the sound of the *Hoochim* podcast aligns with expected norms—the podcast has a consistent musical opening that helps to frame its sound as professionally produced, as it is common practice for podcasters to use familiar intro music during the show's introduction to provide sonic branding and recognizability. The hosts of *Hoochim* generally deploy a standard introduction, which further contributes to a professional sense of branding. The show is broadcast across a number of digital platforms, including iTunes, SoundCloud, and its own website, which also contains typed transcripts of each podcast to improve accessibility. Their skillful deployment of podcast recording equipment, editing software, and distribution platforms help to showcase the digital literacy and cosmopolitan cultural capital of its hosts. Moreover, it assumes digital literacy on the part of its audience in being able to access and consume the content.

Yet the show can also be understood as shaped by a kind of queer disruptive energy that simultaneously challenges these sonic norms. As with many micro media ventures, the hosts of *Hoochim* are self-taught audio broadcasters and operate without the assistance of a professional sound engineer or producer. While there are many shows with consistent sound quality, there are also shows like "Episode 6: New Year New Me" where only one member of the show is in the studio and the other three are separately calling into a Skype voice chat. The sound quality varies significantly between the voice recorded in the studio and the scratchy, garbled sounds of the women calling in. During "Episode 7: VDay," the host Sandy Oh starts to state the tagline, in which the punchline "everything!" is usually enthusiastically stated in unison by all the members. Yet this moment of unity fails, with Sandy speaking the line on her own and the others joining in a half second too late, their voices crackling across the Skype connection. The hosts pay no attention and continue forward unedited and undeterred; the conversation flows easily across a number of topics and the sound quality is never addressed. While such instances may be common in amateur media, we can also connect the decision of the hosts to allow for mistakes and imperfections to go unchecked to their larger goal of not needing to fit in and align with accepted norms—an orientation that can be seen in other decisions about their sound as well.

The show's opening also can be analyzed for the way that it contributes to the show's sonic meanings. First, the soft *qeej* music that provides the backdrop for their introductory comments has specific resonance within Hmong culture. The *qeej* is a Hmong instrument where the player blows into a set of bamboo pipes and produces a set of sounds that are deeply connected to Hmong oral culture, as each tone corresponds to a Hmong word. A skillful player can use the instrument to communicate speech, and the *qeej* has long played an important role in a wide variety of Hmong cultural events. While the *qeej* was historically an instrument played only by men and is still more commonly taught to boys, the Facebook page for *Hoochim* explains that their intro song is played by a woman *qeej* player, Pa-shie Vang. So the brief moments of *qeej* that can be heard beneath the host's introductory comments are able to communicate both the cultural specificity and deep cultural knowledge represented within this Hmong show, as well as a contestation of Hmong cultural norms and gender expectations. Raechel Tiffe and Melody Hoffman (2017) argue that hegemonic vocal norms have always contributed to the policing of women's "deviant voices," and this podcast additionally considers the way that Hmong culture has shaped the gendering of certain sounds. Together with the erratically mixed array of voices that are often calling in from as far away as Laos and Thailand, the sound of the podcast itself conveys a variety of contradictory meanings.

The resistant sound of the show is also mirrored in the way that the hosts speak, the content they choose to discuss, and the particular political stances that they take up. In terms of language, they speak American English with only a smattering of Hmong/Hmonglish. They also unabashedly deploy a colorful variety of curses—including the Episode 11 title, "It's All Fucked Up." In the midst of a conversation about Hmong representation in Hollywood (the specific content is not important), one member stated the following: "All I have to say is fuck those guys. Like fuck 'em. They come into these spaces like, I know who you're talking about but I ain't gonna say that person's name. They come into these spaces and fuckin' preach and preach and preach. Get pissed when they don't get invited. Get pissed when they're not a part of certain conversation about a certain event but yet here they are fucking selling and commodifying our fucking culture." While the show is full of uproarious laughter and sarcasm, there are plenty of moments like this of righteous anger where cursing is used to strengthen the emotion behind their words. One member admitted that after her brother listened to the show, he asked if she could please use fewer curse words, but the hosts are confident and unapologetic about their choice of language.

The topics that the podcast covers are also specifically focused on challenging dominant narratives from other Hmong media outlets, or from what the hosts have seen being talked about in Hmong Facebook groups. As one host stated, "There's a certain narrative that's being said in the community, and since we had a different view, we felt that since our view was the minority, let's find a platform that will let us share the minority view so that all views are out there for people to dissect." This can mean gentle ribbing about Hmong norms through making jokes, such as their running joke about #firsthmong. Their use of this phrase calls attention to the rampant practice among Hmong Americans who lay claim to titles such as "first Hmong to earn a PhD," "first Hmong judge," or "first Hmong nursing graduate student." The hosts of *Hoochim* point out that these claims are not necessarily premised on doing research to establish the veracity of these titles, as other "first Hmong" may have simply failed to document their primacy in a given arena. Moreover, one host gently pointed out that these titles "glorify the person, rather than the content or the reasons why you're in that position." They admit that in many ways, they are also likely "first Hmong" themselves—they host the first Hmong women's podcast, and one of their members who was the first Hmong to attend Yale. Yet their jokes around this common Hmong phraseology serve to identify a norm and call it into question, asking specifically how it might serve to obscure diverse participation or overlook those who have been silenced within their own community.

Their critiques can be much more serious as well, such as when they host conversations about rape, domestic violence, polygamy, and anti-Blackness. In "Episode 4: The New Model Minority Mutiny," the women explore the topic of anti-Blackness in Hmong communities. They discuss the reaction that they have seen within their own families and friend groups where Hmong Americans are opposed to Black Lives Matter activism and its disruptive methods. Linda Her stated, "People are saying Black folks should protest like Dr. Martin Luther King and Gandhi or these nonviolence protest but these Hmong people, when in your life have you actually fucking protested? When have you actually got angry about the discrimination of Hmong people and did something? You have no experience about critical race and history and you take a chapter out of the book that you learned from white schools, how white teachers and white textbooks history tells you about the white people want us to hear about their legacy and their forefathers." They discuss the lack of education within Hmong communities about histories of slavery and the oppression of African Americans, and their feeling that they would like to contribute to more open conversations about the harms of anti-Blackness. Sandy Oh asserts, "This is a battle I want to pick. I want to engage in these conversations with them and I want to understand. And I want them to see it from you know different perspective and I want them to get outside of what they're seeing." They also reflect on their own process of becoming aware of their own Hmong subjectivity in relation to whiteness, and the development of the critical race lens that they now deploy to understand the racial dynamics around them. They recall that it was not easy, and that sometimes it can be scary to be aligned with those who are protesting those in power, such as the police. Yet they are committed to helping their own community grow and develop a stronger anti-racist consciousness, even if it may be difficult.

These choices clearly position the hosts of *Hoochim* as unruly women who are not afraid to challenge convention, and the marginality of their position helps to identify the norms and boundaries of Hmong hegemonic culture that are upheld through other Hmong media. They recognized the possibilities afforded by micro media to create their own program and distribute it online among other Hmong social media, where it can be discussed and debated within their community. As bell hooks (2015) argues, marginality is not a site of deprivation, but "the site of radical possibility, a space of resistance. . . . It offers the possibility of radical perspectives from which to see and create, to imagine alternatives, new worlds" (343). They do not need to seek approval from media gatekeepers or please a team of producers, editors, or marketing teams—as with all micro media creators, they are able to broadcast their unfiltered messages without undergoing these evaluative or potentially stifling processes. This does not mean that they escape social censure, as we can see that they do face criticism within their own community in a way that parallels the negative chatter surrounding Hmong teleconference radio programs. But this does not dampen their conviction or their desire to disrupt hegemonic Hmong American narratives. Linda Her described the problem they seek to address: "There are a lot of Hmong leaders and institutions and people who have a lot of power who can influence, but they're not connecting what is Hmongness to the outer world. It's just very isolated. We want to have a Hmong voice and experience in America that's very connected to what's presently happening and not frozen in time, connected to the war and what happened in 1975." They recognize the strength of their elders and the struggles they have endured, but also want to move past a stasis that can lock their community into problematic ways of thinking and behaving. As women, queer folks, and activists, they recognize the blind spots within hegemonic Hmong and Hmong American culture that often serve to punish those who are most vulnerable and powerless. They are willing to risk the critique and community disapproval that come with media production in order to enter into the media landscape and challenge these power dynamics.

Nplooj Radio

While the hosts of *Hoochim* insert Hmong voices into the podcast landscape, there have been other attempts to reach younger Hmong American and queer audiences with audio media. The radio show *Nplooj* broadcast on WIXK 1590 AM/103.3 FM every other Wednesday from 7:30 to 8:30 P.M. central time from 2016 to 2019. Listeners could tune in through AM/FM radio receivers in the western Wisconsin and Twin Cities region, smartphone apps like the iHeart-Radio app, and websites including tunein.com and mytuner-radio.com. The station's only youth-oriented program, *Nplooj* was cohosted by Sonic Rain, Chuefeng Xiong, and Cameron Yang. Sonic and Cameron identify as queer trans Hmong, and Chuefeng identifies as a straight cisgender Hmong man. Chuefeng's participation served to model allyship and open up a point of connection and identification for straight cisgender listeners. As Sonic explains, "There's such a toxic masculinity that Hmong men revolve around. The fact that Chuefeng is here as a cis straight ally with two queer trans Hmong folks, other straight cis Hmong men can be friends and accept this too. That's why it's super important and necessary that he's here." For their weekly hour-long broadcast, they played contemporary Hmong pop music and chatted with guests, who included Hmong and Hmong American artists, activists, and entrepreneurs. The show was explicitly themed around Hmong LGBTQIA+ (a term that includes lesbian, gay, bisexual, trans, queer, intersexed, asexual, agender, and other identities) issues and identities, but the conversations were wide ranging and did not always focus on sexuality or queer issues. The tone was a blend of silly playfulness and more heartfelt conversations, and was primarily in English language with some Hmong spoken on occasion.

While the sounds of *Hoochim* can be seen to queer and challenge the Hmong aural landscape, the radio show *Nplooj* strived for a more consistently professional sound. This effort aligns with the goals of Hmong Radio WIKX more broadly. As mentioned in the previous chapter, this radio station is noteworthy because it was the first Hmong AM/FM radio station to be owned and operated by a Hmong American woman. Since 2014, Mai Yia Yang has owned the station and broadcast out of a facility in St. Paul. As with all of the forms of Hmong radio described in this book, the station clearly falls into the category of micro media industry, with only Yang, her son, and a part-time engineer serving as paid staff. In an effort to reach a younger audience, Mai Yia Yang approached her other child, Cameron Yang (who goes by Cam and uses they/them pronouns), about the possibility of becoming a radio host. Cam was in college and had come out as queer and gender nonconforming four years earlier. Although Mai Yia and her husband were surprised about these identities at first, they had slowly been growing more supportive and accepting over time. Cam agreed to do the show, but did not let on that the topic would be LGBTQIA+ themed. Cam recruited friends Sonic Rain and Chuefeng to join in hosting, and *Nplooj* was born. After the show premiered and there was indeed a boost in their targeted youth audience, Mai Yia Yang eventually accepted the topic as an important component of the station's weekly lineup.

While the content of the show pushes some boundaries, Mai Yia Yang is clear about her concerns that the station more generally always needs to conform to the mandates established by the FCC. When asked about her managerial style when meeting with her DJs, she affirmed that she is always reminding them about FCC rules such as not swearing and sticking to the facts when talking about the news. Although she had never run into problems with the FCC, she feared potential consequences. Given the reality that all micro media industries are vulnerable due to multiple overlapping factors, this additional threat of the FCC looking over their shoulder loomed large even if the actual possibility of censure remained marginal. Moreover, as the sole woman running a radio station, she worried about the reputation of the station among the Hmong community. She was proud that her radio station was on the AM dial because it represented a degree of professionalism in comparison to the teleconference radio stations. But she recognized that Hmong women's voices were often dismissed and went unrecognized, and did not want her radio station to suffer this fate.

Amid this environment of careful professionalism, the hosts of *Nplooj* nevertheless made a number of deliberate queer interventions. First, they openly called attention to their queer Hmong identities and discussed issues of importance to the LGBTQIA+ Hmong American community. Cam discussed the importance of representation for the hosts: "In our spare time we do go out and get political and volunteer, but it's important to have a radio show because the API [Asian Pacific Islander] Hmong community isn't represented enough in media. That's why we're trying to take this extra step to use radio to show we're Hmong, we're queer, we're here." They also invited queer guests onto the program, such as their March 7, 2018, show where Maysa Vang and Mindy Yang participated in *Nplooj*'s discussion series on the topic of toxic masculinity. Vang and Yang are the creators of a YouTube vlog called *Black Crane* where they chat and joke about their experiences as Hmong lesbians. On the *Nplooj* program they discussed their experiences struggling against the socially constructed labels of "man" and "woman" in the Hmong community, and in their families. Yang talked about growing up as a tomboy and being harassed for enjoying traditionally masculine hobbies like fixing cars and fishing. They also discussed their frustration with the way that straight men sexualized lesbians with feminine gender expression, at times disrespecting their queer partners.

One of the norms of the LGBTQIA+ community that the hosts of *Nplooj* deployed regularly on the show is having their guests introduce themselves by giving their names and their gender pronouns. Some of their cisgender Hmong guests may have been unfamiliar with this practice, but the hosts worked to create new queer norms around what it meant to participate in their aural space. They also developed a way to disrupt the hegemonic norms of radio by broadcasting simultaneous video recordings of their sessions on Facebook through the live video feature. They described their decision as based on a desire to be innovative and help start new trends, but also to make it accessible for their target audience to listen and watch. Live video had been introduced to the Facebook platform in August 2015, and many Hmong were starting to use it to connect with viewers.

In some ways, these Facebook Live broadcasts challenge our understanding of radio as a medium in the same way that other micro media industries challenge accepted boundaries through hybrid media platforms. While podcasts and other streaming media can be accessed at any time that is convenient for the consumer, radio programs have traditionally only been available through over-the-air transmissions broadcast live. With the advent of web streaming "radio on the internet," there has been debate about what qualities constitute "radioness" alongside converging media technologies that often allow for time-shifted listening practices (Freire 2007). Some of the Hmong radio broadcasts discussed in chapter 4 are archived and made available online, for at least a short amount of time. This is particularly true for the many once-a-week Hmong shows produced for community radio stations, as it has become common for community radio shows to make their most recent programming available online as podcasts for a week or two. But the mediation of *Nplooj* further complicates these typologies through their production of transmediated radio broadcasts in which audience members choose between two flows of content— the first option is audio broadcast on the AM/FM dial (or via a radio app), and the second option is the audiovisual stream available on Facebook's website or mobile app.

These two sources offer both different technological affordances as well as different content, despite their simultaneity. For instance, the radio program offers an audio broadcast for hands-free listening while driving, and the majority of the program is focused on listening to Hmong music. In contrast, the Facebook platform displays the bodies and faces of the hosts amid the studio setting, and music breaks are taken as an opportunity to speak freely to one another, dance and laugh, and take care of logistical needs. Indeed, breaking into spontaneous dance parties while giggling uncontrollably was a regular feature of the music breaks for Facebook fans to enjoy. At a basic level, those who want to hear music would listen to the audio broadcast, while those who want to see the interactions of the hosts would tune into Facebook. There are other small differences as well, such as that the DJs tell guests they are not allowed to swear during the radio broadcast (due to FCC regulations emphasized earlier) but can say whatever they want when the mics are turned off and they are only speaking to their Facebook Live video audience. This act of code-switching between a somewhat professional radio performance and what might be understood as a more uninhibited video performance calls attention to the limits of more traditional broadcasting platforms. We can see how their video platform more directly centers the hosts themselves, visually showcasing their genderqueer fashion and style choices while also facilitating direct interaction with their online commenters.

This use of multiple broadcasting technologies also reveals the realities of how micro media industries operate. While it may be difficult or even impossible for listeners tuning into the audio stream of radio on the AM/FM dial to understand everyone who is involved in producing the segment, the size of the studio and number of participants becomes perfectly visible through the Facebook video feed. Those who have the opportunity to watch Chuefeng taking control of the computer monitor, Sonic Rain slipping on a pair of headphones to speak into the microphone, and Cam ushering the guest into a seat realize that there are no producers, engineers, or other staff supporting the show.

On a different day, I sat in the studio while station owner Mai Yia Yang hosted her show without any video broadcast, as is the norm for her. During one music break, she pushed play on the song and then turned to me and said, "People think that when they listen to it, they think it must be very fun at the radio! But it's just one person and all this equipment, it's lonely in here. They always think there's people in here, but it's just yourself." This is the reality for many micro media producers—that their process of media creation is solitary and isolating, without any opportunity for social interaction or collaboration. Yet the *Nplooj* show is notable for openly revealing their challenge to that norm. They may be personally responsible for every aspect of the show's operation, but that means that they are also fully in control of how they are represented and what kind of media they want to produce. In Kong Pheng Pha's (2016) exploration of queer Hmong America, he asks if it is even possible for queer Hmong Americans to be happy. Indeed, the persistent focus on the struggles of LGBTQ+ people within Hmong culture makes it difficult to imagine an alternative. But *Nplooj* provides an exuberant, affectionate response to this question by broadcasting their queer Hmong American joy, friendships, and community on a weekly basis.

Hmong Musical Artists

This conversation about Hmong radio also provides an opportunity to consider its relationship to Hmong musical artists, many of whom are also operating outside of mainstream music industries in their own form of micro media. The hosts of *Nplooj* noted that they often struggled to find queer Hmong musicians to highlight on their show, as there were very few queer Hmong artists who were out and ready to share their music. Nonetheless, they were excited that they were able to feature a diverse variety of contemporary Hmong artists from their local community and around the world, including hip hop, acoustic, rock, funk, ballads, and pop songs. Since both Sonic Rain and Chuefeng worked in the music industry, they were often able to rely on their inside connections to learn about local artists and help provide a platform for them. Their focus on Hmong musical artists reveals yet another site for considering how micro media industries operate by creating symbiotic relationships between multiple forms of micro media.

Gary Yia Lee (2006) dates the origins of modern Hmong music to end of the Vietnam War in 1975, when Hmong gained access to new musical instruments in the refugee camps. Previous Hmong musical traditions were based around the voice and culturally specific instruments such as the *qeej* (reed pipe), the *raj* (flute), or the *ncas* (mouth harp). With the sharing of Hmong culture throughout the diaspora via cassette tapes, VHS videos, and CDs, Hmong singers were able to develop and spread new Hmong music that was infused with styles from Thailand, Laos, or the Western sounds of rock and pop for those who had resettled in United States. Louisa Schein (2002) describes this blossoming of Hmong American music in the late 1970s: "Teenagers and twenty-something Hmong purchased rudimentary electric instruments and amplifiers and churned out blaring sounds . . . and the majority concern the time-honored themes of romance and heartbreak" (235). Hmong musicians were able to cultivate a kind of transnational stardom that was based on connecting nostalgically to the dream of a lost Hmong homeland while also adapting to contemporary musical styles. There are now dozens of Hmong bands and musical artists who can fill stadiums with thousands of fans and are constantly churning out new songs and albums.

If micro media industries are defined by the small number of individuals involved in developing, creating, and distributing professional media content, Hmong musical artists are certainly in this category. The terms "independent music" or "indie" are used to describe both an aesthetic genre of music and a political alternative to the corporate recording industry for artists seeking more creative and financial control (Hesmondhalgh 1999). The rise of indie music can be viewed as a response to the rapid consolidation of the commercial music industry that led to the majority of music being produced by only three major record labels—Universal Music Group, Sony Music Entertainment, and Warner Music Group. There are a handful of Hmong record labels in the United States that identify as independent, such as Yellow Diamond Records, Deevsiab Records, and Evolution Records Entertainment. Yet independent music encompasses an extremely wide swath of artists and corporations, and many independent record labels are neither fully divested from nor positioned in opposition to major record labels. As with the category of "independent film," there is room for the avant-garde, the micro, and the radical alongside those operating under a set of industrial norms that look remarkably similar to the mainstream.

At another level, the rise of independent music has also been facilitated by the increasing accessibility of music technologies and tools that allow for DIY and amateur production and distribution. Kembrew McLeod (2005) describes the opportunities available for individual musicians and independent artist-entrepreneurs to record their own music at home and distribute it online for free. Using music editing software such as GarageBand, Pro Tools, or Audacity, prosumers can then upload their audio tracks and music videos to social media networks such as YouTube, Facebook, and SoundCloud, or sites such as ehmongmusic.com that share Hmong mp3s. The vast majority of Hmong musicians and bands fall into this category, rather than having been signed by even an independent record label. Many artists perform at live venues such as Hmong New Year, open mics, or local festivals, but maintain full-time jobs outside of the music world. Some self-produced artists name their own "micro-label" when they publish their music online in an act of self-branding that connects the Hmong music industry to other micro music industries discussed throughout this book.

We can thus see how Hmong radio stations and Hmong independent artists have a symbiotic relationship. Unlike commercial radio stations that are limited to playing commercial hits produced by the major record labels, Hmong radio stations have the freedom to highlight a wide range of Hmong artists. In this way they are similar to college campus radio stations and community radio, both of which have a history of focusing on noncommercial music. Hmong radio stations play everything from traditional Hmong songs from the 1980s and 1990s to contemporary popular songs released by Hmong record labels to performances by amateurs who mail their CDs or email their MP3 files to DJs. Given that these musical artists often operate alone, occupy a precarious professional position, and are not necessarily supported by a record label, they are often more than happy to be invited to visit a radio station and chat with the hosts about their music. When *Nplooj* invites its weekly guests to come onto their show, introduce themselves and their preferred gender pronouns, and then engage in warm, friendly conversation with its young Hmong American hosts, these independent artists also participate in normalizing the LGBTQA+ positioning of the show itself. This particular relationship reveals the salience of connections and relationships across different micro media industries, as well as the role that they can play in amplifying support for each other and the positions they hold.

Poj Laib / Bad Hmong Girl

In addition to *Nplooj*, the radio show *HmongFM* on KFAI 90.3 FM in the Twin Cities is another more traditional radio format that has also been deployed as a way to call attention to queer issues in the Hmong American community. *HmongFM* was hosted by Kathy Mouacheupao and Wameng Moua for eleven years from 2006 to 2017. The weekly two-hour program combined contemporary Hmong music with commentary and discussion with the hosts and guests. One of the hosts, Kathy Mouacheupao, was a longtime supporter of the queer Hmong organization SOY and often invited queer guests, artists, and musicians to share the microphone. But the show became a more explicit space for this conversation in August 2017, with the premiere of a six-part series called *Poj Laib / Bad Hmong Girl*. Each week they featured a different set of guests to talk about what the term "*poj laib*" meant to them, and more generally how they understood gender inequities in the Hmong community. The series also featured live broadcasts of a new radio play written by May Lee-Yang that tackled issues about Hmong womanhood. This program further contributed to the queer radio archive discussed throughout this chapter by connecting issues of Hmong gender (and specifically womanhood) to the issue of queer sexuality, while also revealing another kind of innovation that is facilitated through micro media—the possibility to expand media genres, such as through experimenting with Hmong dramatic performances and storytelling rather than adhering to a more conventional radio call-in format.

In the first episode of *Poj Laib*, Kathy Mouacheupao invited Hmong fashion artist and queer activist Oskar Ly to be her cohost. Oskar described her desire to "queer up the conversation" by inviting other participants who identified in different ways with regard to gender and sexuality: Bo Thao-Uribe, Joann Van Buuren, and the two queer hosts from *Nplooj*, Sonic Rain and Cameron Yang. They opened the discussion with an explanation of how they understood the term "*poj laib*" or "bad Hmong girl" as a term for Hmong girls and women who break from social norms of idealized femininity. This includes a wide range of activities, including but not limited to staying out late (even to work on school projects), dying their hair, being lazy, sleeping in, advocating for themselves, being independent, having aspirations outside the home, being bad wives or daughters-in-law, and getting divorced. Yet they also affirmed that many Hmong women gravitated toward the term and embraced it, working to reclaim the negative and derogatory term into a badge of pride.

The first show specifically interrogated the way that issues of gender identity and femininity intersected with sexuality in the families and communities of the guests. Oskar Ly explained that she had been called a "*poj laib*" many times by her mother, but that when she came out as a lesbian it seemed that term did not apply anymore because she no longer fit into ideal Hmong womanhood at all. Bruce Thao (2016) discusses the intersectional struggles facing queer Hmong women who challenge norms around proper Hmong femininity and womanhood. As he states, Hmong lesbian, bisexual, and queer women are displaced due to the way they "[complicate] and [challenge] the male-female gender binary and traditional gender roles. The impact of such dislocation is exacerbated for queer Hmong, for whom displacement within queer communities is compounded by the Hmong's history of geographic displacement" (292).

The conversation between Kathy Mouacheupao and her guests was then followed by the first part of a radio drama called *The Poj Laib Project*. It was written by Hmong playwright May Lee-Yang, and had been commissioned by Mouacheupao to thematically accompany the conversations. As a former executive director of the Center for Hmong Arts and Talent, Mouacheupao had been a longtime advocate for Hmong theater and other art forms. She served as the narrator for the seven-minute story, which relayed what she called an unfortunately all-too-common tale for a young Hmong couple—after the wife gives birth to ten children, the husband starts to feel neglected and has an affair with a younger woman. The younger woman gets pregnant and demands that he marry her, which turns both women into *poj laib*. The first wife is shamed for refusing to allow her husband a second wife in spite of being too busy to make him happy, and the girlfriend for becoming an outcast because she was impregnated without getting married.

The radio broadcast of *The Poj Laib Project* stands out as the kind of bold and innovative programming choice that is made possible through the flexibility and adaptability of micro media formats. Radio dramas proliferated in the early days of the medium, with programs like *Amos 'n' Andy* and Orson Welles's *The War of the Worlds*. Yet they have become increasingly rare in the decades since then, as narrative storytelling moved to television and radio was primarily used for music and nonfiction broadcasting. In modern times, narrative radio has seen a resurgence in podcast form, but it is still rare for terrestrial broadcasts to include narrative or dramatic content. Like the other forms of micro media we have seen exemplified in this book, this small program on a community radio station offered its hosts the chance to create media that was culturally specific and meaningful to its small audience. For Hmong Americans, oral storytelling has long been the primary way to communicate cultural values and norms in the absence of a written history, as was discussed in chapter 4 with regard to the rise of Hmong teleconference radio programs. While oral cultures use the repetition of time-worn folktales and narratives to sustain their culture, *The Poj Laib Project* uses this familiar format to help create new narratives of change and disruption. May Lee-Yang's stories use humor to gently criticize the way that Hmong women are subjugated through practices such as polygamy and assumptions that independent women are bad.

In the conversation that follows the radio drama, the guests on *HmongFM* discuss these different meanings of the story. Sonic Rain first responds with laughter, remarking on how much she relates to the story in her own life: "It's so funny, I love the way she writes comedy . . . I'm a man! Whatever I say, she gonna obey! It hits me . . . that's how it is." Mouacheupao comments that it always strikes her when women respond to the play with laughter, because they are actually laughing at the demise and sorrow of these women and "the crap that happens in our community." Although the play is written as humorous satire, it is clearly discussing serious problems. She states: "There's an English word for this . . . this is straight-up abuse. This is abusive, and something we don't want to talk about, and that we've normalized . . . I know of women who are blamed and shamed, they're constantly revictimized and sent back." This discussion reveals some of the ways that *HmongFM* uses multiple genres within audio media to help queer Hmong women and allies lead the way in reframing conversations about gender and sexuality.

The other five episodes of the series did not feature queer women or center conversations about the place of queer sexualities within the construct of the "good Hmong girl." Yet as the kickoff for the entire series, this conversation served as the foundation for the episodes that followed. It established the definition of "*poj laib*" to which the other guests would return again and again, and firmly connected gender and sexuality within the discussion. These are some of the ways that Hmong micro media industries make space for marginalized populations to tell their stories and reach broader audiences, as well as for hosting conversations that model different affective responses to stories of oppression that are quite painful to hear. The flexibility of genre that is afforded to these outlets provides space for creating new artistic expression and challenges to our expectations of radio and what it can do.

Producing a Queer Audio Archive

If these discussions by and about queer, gender nonconforming, and otherwise unruly Hmong women are designed to challenge mainstream Hmong culture, one of the questions we might ask is about the size of their audience. The social impact of media is obviously limited if the content is difficult to access or targeted to a tiny audience. Both of these factors are relevant for many Hmong micro media industries, and radio in particular is often an ephemeral product that demands live listening in order to consume at all. Yet this does not mean that archives and sustained engagement are impossible; on the contrary, all three of the programs examined here deliberately work to create archives of their audio programming. Not only do these stable repositories make it so audiences can time-shift their listening practices to fit into their schedules, but they also greatly expand the potential audience who might be able to locate and access the programs years after they broadcast. This is particularly important for Hmong audiences who have widely varying levels of access to online technologies, as well as digital literacy, and may not be able to communicate news about programming effectively across the diaspora.

The archiving practices of each program are different, given their different technological affordances. As mentioned earlier, the *Nplooj* show records a

Facebook Live audiovisual version of their weekly shows, and these videos are maintained on their Facebook page for time-shifted consumption. The radio station KFAI posts episodes of their programs on its website for two weeks—a time limit that is set according to their musical licensing agreements. It does keep its own digital archive of programs, but it is not publicly available. After producing the series *Poj Laib* during *HmongFM*'s final broadcasts, they made the decision to edit out music so they could avoid the rights issue and post links to the show that could be available indefinitely. Because of this, the only *HmongFM* archive that remains online is the *Poj Laib* program. This brief snippet of *HmongFM*'s eleven-year run then places a great amount of value onto this series and its messages—including how to resist Hmong gender norms, as well as the importance of facilitating polyvocal discourse about how to address the problems of gender policing in Hmong culture. This impact was further intensified by the fact that *HmongFM* went off the air following the last broadcast of the *Poj Laib* series. Not only was this series the only one that could be indefinitely hosted on KFAI's website, but it was also the literal last word from *HmongFM*.

The *Hoochim* podcast is even more robustly archived due to the affordances of podcasts themselves. While all digital files are inherently ephemeral and in danger of becoming obsolete, corrupted, or inaccessible, there are some benefits to the podcast format with regard to archival possibilities. The audio files that comprise podcasts are distributed digitally via different platforms (Sound-Cloud, iTunes, Stitcher, etc.), where they can be downloaded to each individual user's computer or audio player. This means that rather than relying on the podcasters themselves to host the files, there is some redundancy within the different podcast distribution platforms. Mel Hogan (2009) has argued that the technical affordances of podcasts have helped lesbian and queer women to take ownership over their own audio history. She states: "It is podcasting's intrinsic archival potential, as I define herein, which characterizes it as a tool for activism. I propose that podcasting is a powerful participatory alternative to both traditional radio programming and traditional means of recording, organizing and preserving collections" (200). The ease with which podcast creators can distribute their own messages helps their reach to grow, even decades after the content was originally created. This is good news for the creators of *Hoochim*, who certainly would like to see their audience expand over time. But they have also taken additional measures to expand their own archive by producing text transcriptions of each podcast episode. This is an enormous undertaking by volunteers, with some of their hour-long podcasts resulting in transcriptions that are over 14,000 words long. Yet the expanded reach and uses for this are immense, as it means that audiences can access their content even if they are hearing-impaired or do not have the ability to listen. It also means that their podcasts have the affordances of digital text, such as searchability by researchers and improved search engine optimization that can increase visibility within web search engines. These are some of the many ways that micro media outlets are able to extend their reach and overcome some of the limitations that might otherwise make it difficult for content to be accessed, particularly when their content is already designed for a small audience.

Conclusion: Adapting Audio Media for Cultural Change

These queer Hmong audio programs can clearly be seen to challenge some of the dominant norms of the Hmong diasporic media landscape. There is often considerable pressure on Hmong media producers to conform to expectations around addressing audiences in traditional ways and reproducing a kind of Hmong respectability politics amid a struggle for this small population to gain legibility and authority. The unabashedly unruly hosts of these programs remind us that this kind of assimilation is not the only path to empowerment, and in fact harms those who cannot align with these norms, or who refuse to. As Hmong culture itself changes and evolves in response to new cultural and technological contexts, programs such as these point to new opportunities for using media to support some of the most vulnerable communities.

This exploration of the way that radio and other forms of audio media remain meaningful and relevant even to young Hmong American media producers reminds us that media cultures reflect the diversity of experiences within Hmong American communities. The previous chapter examined the development of Hmong teleconference radio as a way for Hmong across the diaspora to merge audio technologies with digital platforms as a way of addressing one set of needs—an oral form of participatory communication that could be accessed 24/7 on low-tech cell phones. But the Hmong American radio and podcast producers from this chapter have an entirely different set of needs and identifications—they are seeking out a space that allows them to express their full identities (including gender and sexual identities), access the cultural capital of popular emerging technologies like podcasting, integrate their voices and stories with music, and articulate support for their own visions of cultural change. While both of these chapters provide an examination of audio media and different forms of radio, it is clear that they are addressing different Hmong American identities and experiences, and the media expressions that result are also very different.

Whether they are chatting with peers, podcasting, supplementing broadcast radio signals with Facebook Live video feeds, or using their community radio station to amplify the voices of youth activists, Hmong Americans are clearly finding ways to engage with audio media that make sense to them. In the next chapter, we dig deeper into the digital lives of Hmong American youth with an investigation of influencers and content creators who are thriving in the digital realm of social media. Like the creative and innovative audio media producers explored in this chapter, Hmong influencers also have worked to develop a unique voice that is recognizable to their fans and audience members. But as we will see, the norms of the influencer world are already aligned with micro media entrepreneurship in ways that challenge the expectations of the Hmong Americans who are simply seeking to grow as media producers.

6

Alternative
Aspirational Labor

· ·

Influencers and Social
Media Producers

It was the middle of the summer, and Hmong American college student Phillipe Thao was having trouble focusing on the paper he needed to write for his math course. He decided to open an Excel spreadsheet and put together a definitive ranking of every song by Hilary Duff. After two hours of working on it, he screenshotted the spreadsheet and posted it on Twitter, where it quickly started accumulating likes and retweets. His obsession with Hilary Duff was particularly celebrated within the gay Twitter community in which he was an active member, and the post ended up discussed in a Babe.net article titled "This guy—no, this LEGEND—ranked every Hilary Duff song instead of writing a 15-page paper." Phillipe Thao had gone viral.

With his sharp wit, fashionable look, and consistently incisive analysis relayed through 280-character messages on Twitter, this sudden burst of internet fame was nothing new to Thao. Since joining Twitter in high school, he had accumulated a steadily growing following, and was already experiencing the effects of micro-celebritydom at his college. As he said to me in an interview, "Literally every party I went to, there would be someone I didn't know who would say, I don't want to be awkward around you but I follow you on Twitter. Or they would message me afterward and say, I didn't want to approach you because you seem so intimidating." Outside of his Twitter account, he also

119

had a popular Instagram account filled with magazine-worthy shots of artisanal donuts, self-portraits set against murals, and Chicago's skyscrapers. He felt pressure to keep his social media feeds open so he could stay on top of the latest posts, but it also paid off on occasion—like when an editor at *Teen Vogue* wrote to Thao about one of his tweets on the release of *Crazy Rich Asians* and invited him to expand it into a full article.

We have seen throughout the book the way that digital media have allowed Hmong Americans to produce a wide array of traditional media, such as newspapers, television, and radio, while also developing a range of hybrid media platforms. Within this small ethnic community, media formats that are traditionally staffed by dozens (if not hundreds) of paid workers must be scaled down to an extremely limited staff size. Yet the rise of social media has facilitated the development of a kind of media entrepreneurship that is already focused at the level of the individual. On platforms like YouTube, Instagram, Twitter, Facebook, and others, there are thousands of enterprising individuals who have risen to fame and fortune by crafting a mediated presence that centers their unique voice. In cases such as these, the media texts themselves are less important than the individual behind the creations, and qualities such as authenticity, voice, and self-branding are emphasized as the key to how one person can become a successful media entrepreneur without any connection to mainstream media industries. Yet the existence of these digital superstars represents a fundamental shift from the Hmong micro media industries investigated thus far, given that we have primarily seen entrepreneur-owners striving to foreground a corporate or organizational identity rather than their individual identity. The newspapers, television stations, radio stations, and YouTube channels investigated in the previous chapters often disguise how few individuals are actually laboring behind the scenes, as if it were a flaw to conceal. Social media influencers oftentimes attract a following by foregrounding the singular personality and voice of their star—sometimes even strategically concealing any team of support staff or institutional cooptation that are actually present.

This chapter explores Hmong American social media producers and influencers who have large followings on a variety of digital platforms in order to further expand on the notion of the self-made media entrepreneur. It is based on an examination of fifteen Hmong American social media accounts with followers ranging from six thousand to seventy thousand. My findings are supplemented with interviews I conducted with three individuals, as well as analysis of online videos capturing interviews with Hmong American influencers.[1] I ask how Hmong Americans fit into the scholarship on social media influencers, but also how the rise of influencers challenges and expands the category of micro media industries. This chapter reveals the fact that individuals with limited audiences and resources fall prey to many of the same struggles that all influencers and micro media entrepreneurs face, which helps us to see new connections between categories like ethnic media and digital superstardom. Yet these Hmong American influencers discuss the way that their digital micro-celebritydom becomes personally significant beyond the drive toward capitalization and growth that is assumed to be central to the work of being an influencer. Here we see that the lessons we have learned about micro media entrepreneurship are aligned with the labor that all social media influencers take on and the struggles they face, but that the category of social media entrepreneurship can also be expanded to include those whose hardships and benefits are not connected to desire for monetization.

Influencers as Media Producers

The title of "influencer" is used to describe individuals who have large, loyal followings on social media platforms. The term originated within the business world of marketing and advertising, as these influential individuals could be hired to make personally meaningful endorsements of corporate brands and products to consumers. We have always understood that celebrities have the power to shift opinion, culture, and purchasing decisions, traditionally having gained fame through participating in mainstream media industries and mass culture. Yet with the rise of blogging and other forms of social media, everyday citizens also began to gain a smaller degree of this same power and sway. Crystal Abidin (2018) emphasizes that there is now a distinction between this business-related use of the term "influencer" and a more vernacular, cultural usage, where individuals pursue "a vocation and practice focused on social media-based, multimedia, fame on the internet" (72). Today's social media influencers accrue audiences from writing and creating posts, sharing images, tweeting, making videos, or otherwise deploying the affordances of online tools that invite media creation.

This description of labor is fitting for many Hmong American social media users who have become popular through focusing on a topic such as fashion, food, travel, beauty, or fitness. Like many forms of micro media enterprise, their ability to gain audiences is directly connected to the potentials of Web 2.0, or the shift in digital platforms from static pages toward those that center on allowing users to create and share content. Social media sites like Facebook and Twitter are free to join, and they gain value from amassing thousands of users who collectively participate in producing and making decisions about how to share content. Yet research on influencers points to how this reliance on digital platforms has also shaped the way that social media users see themselves and others. As Theresa Senft (2013) argues, the architectures of these digital platforms allow and encourage users to surveil and judge one another's content, which in turn transforms one's online presence into a performance of the self.

Further, when the purpose of the internet moved toward e-commerce and the market-based activities of production, distribution, and consumption, internet users started to view themselves and their identities through the lens of capitalist logics. The term "micro-celebrity" then is used to describe more than a small degree of fame, but also the way that individuals become well known to a niche audience through creating a unified, branded version of the self that appeals to their online fans. Alice Marwick (2015) defines micro-celebrity not by simply who someone is, but what one does—which includes practices such as interacting with fans, strategically disclosing intimate details in order to appear "authentic," and consistently engaging in self-promotion in order to increase one's social status.

The close relationship between these individuals and the corporations who have come to depend on them for promotional purposes is often viewed critically, as the authenticity of these individuals is exploited for its ability to shore up already powerful institutions. While the affordances, infrastructures, and business models of Web 2.0 have been celebrated for their role in democratizing media production and promoting the voices and marginalized perspectives of everyday citizens, the realities of influencers as micro-celebrities points to some of the ways in which these potentials are often overstated. Elizabeth Bird (2011) reminds us that there has been much attention and praise given to the rise of "produsers" who blur boundaries between consumers and producers. But relatively few individuals actually participate in these activities, and mainstream media industries have responded by disciplining, co-opting, and profiting from that labor. In some cases where it appears that an everyday media user has managed to rise to viral fame, the reality is that they are already being supported by professional media industries—meaning that the maintenance of a home-made aesthetic and narrative of struggle are insincere. Abidin (2017a) terms the staging of this kind of content "calibrated amateurism," marking the frequency with which amateurism can be symbolically produced even amid an increasingly professionalized industry. As a result, Bird concludes we may have over-emphasized the potential for these audiences-turned-produsers to actually shift power dynamics within traditional media hierarchies.

Beyond concerns about deception, another reality that serves to distance social media influencers from everyday media users is the rise of social media influencer agencies. Abidin (2017b) traces the rise of these talent agencies in Singapore to 2007, when management firms started facilitating contractual relationships between brands and influencers. While the global norms around these agencies vary, the existence of many such firms in the United States and elsewhere amid a general shift toward the professionalization of influencer labor exacerbate differences between the haves and the have-nots of influencers—that is, between influencers and micro-influencers (or micro-micro-influencers). The distinction between macro-influencers and micro-influencers is primarily based on size—macro-influencers have social media followings ranging from one hundred thousand to millions of followers, while micro-influencers have smaller followings of one thousand to twenty thousand followers (with a blurry middle ground somewhere in between). This distinction marks the way that influencers may appear to be self-made, self-managed individual workers, but the reality is that their social media production may be professionally managed and directed by corporate interests.

Together these studies of influencers and micro-celebrities help us to better understand what is at stake in investigating the experiences of Hmong American micro-influencers. While it is not hard to find Hmong Americans who create media of some kind, there are very few Hmong Americans who have risen above the social media din and been recognized as influencers. As with all forms of Hmong media production, the limits that constrain audience size mean that Hmong micro-influencers are relatively sheltered from co-optation by established media institutions. The group of Hmong American micro-influencers examined in this chapter do not attract large enough audiences to be able to make a living from corporate sponsorship, and are rarely even approached for this kind of commercial partnership. Yet they nevertheless are understood to wield a measure of some social influence through their media production, and they engage in a set of practices consistent with both micro-celebrity and influencer logics. Even if the number of Hmong American influencers is small and the size of their reach remains relatively limited in comparison to the digital elite who collect millions of views and engagements every day, it is important to consider their existence, the work that they produce, and their potential to impact the small audiences that they do have. Hmong Americans who are using the tools of Web 2.0 for self-promotion, self-branding, and the development of celebrity constitute an important site of media production that contributes to this larger conversation about both user-generated content and Hmong American media industries more broadly. They challenge these new norms where individuals who appear self-made actually are supported by or working to benefit corporate brands and already powerful social media companies, revealing the specific motivations, benefits, and challenges of those who cannot or will not participate in the capitalist logics of social media influencing.

Hmong American Influencers as Micro Media Entrepreneurs

Naomi Kong is a Hmong American hair stylist from the Twin Cities who has actively pursued becoming a fitness influencer. She started her Instagram account in 2017 after carefully surveying the social media landscape and deciding that with so few prominent Asian women in the fitness space, there was room for her to make a name for herself. Kong's Instagram account is her most popular and frequently updated platform, but she also maintains an active

Facebook page and posts videos to YouTube as well. Her posts include brief videos of different workout movements, reviews of activewear fashion, and "fitspiration" posts that explain her own workout journey and encourage others to get moving.

Naomi Kong's social media activities reflect many similarities between influencers and the micro media entrepreneurs examined throughout this book. Just as Hmong American journalists operate newspapers in addition to radio stations and television stations, influencers must also coordinate multiple platforms and are constantly negotiating the differences between them. Naomi Kong explained the differences across her multiple platforms in an interview: "I feel like Instagram is my little baby because that's where I started. The only reason I started a Facebook was to turn my Instagram into a business profile. It's an entire differently audience I can reach, so why not? Instagram is where I'm the most personal, you see the most about my day-to-day life. I feel like that's really where my community is and people can really relate to me and see where I am. Facebook is strictly professional, you don't see my day to day. On YouTube it's all beginner-based [video tutorials]." We can see from this explanation that Instagram, Facebook, and YouTube are understood differently and necessitate different choices about use. They have different audiences who might be drawn to different kinds of content; for instance, Naomi Kong sees her Instagram audience as being more interested in her personal life, while her Facebook offers professional legitimacy and may be where professional contacts are made. There are differences in terms of technological affordances as well, such as the fact that Instagram videos cannot be paused and thus do not provide as helpful of a platform for viewers to watch in the middle of a workout tutorial. Together, we can see that each influencer must become a multimedia content manager, carefully negotiating the ideal content for each platform while also responding to the unique forms of audience interaction that are available on each platform (liking, friending, subscribing, direct messaging, etc.).

There are also many ways in which influencers embody the entrepreneurial identities and drives that we have seen motivate all Hmong American media workers. The relationship between social media influencers and entrepreneurship has been well established, particularly by scholars who are interested in the gendered dimensions of creative production. At a basic level we may want to be careful not to call every social media user an "entrepreneur," given the values ascribed to creativity, innovation, skill development, risk, and business operations in defining entrepreneurial labor. The act of simply posting a photograph online or tweeting comments may not rise to this definition. Yet the labor undertaken by social media influencers also suffers from being consistently overlooked and underestimated. There are multiple overlapping reasons that contribute to this, some of which include: the devalued identities of the young women who do much of this work (Abidin 2016); the emphasis within influencer culture on traditionally feminine areas such as fashion, beauty, cooking, and consumer culture; the struggle that many individuals face in successfully monetizing their social media work or converting it into a sustainable career; and the reputation of this kind of work as "cool" and "glamorous" rather than hard work (Neff, Wissinger, and Zukin 2005). Together these factors have made it easy to downgrade all participation in social media production to merely a frivolous hobby.

But as Duffy and Hund (2015) argue, there are also many social media users who do engage in entrepreneurial labor. They examine how members of this creative workforce often rely on the intense discipline and immaterial labor of self-branding in a way that serves to articulate a new form of self-enterprise. They are concerned with the fact this mode of entrepreneurship centers on a particularly limiting and harmful conception of femininity that includes postfeminist notions of being able to "have it all" while glorifying the rhetoric of choice, independence, and self-expression rooted in consumer culture. Postfeminism is harmful in the way that it rewards individual success when rooted in consumer culture, and celebrates individual worker-subjects taking on all of the responsibilities of self-governance. Indeed, in another article, Duffy (2017a) argues that the kind of online entrepreneurship taken up by women is constrained within a digital double bind that requires traditional forms of femininity and leads to an inferior form of entrepreneurship. Nonetheless, we can clearly see the different ways in which this labor must be understood as entrepreneurial even amid these limits and concerns.

These gendered understandings of influencers as entrepreneurs also emerge within conversations with Hmong American influencers. For instance, Sophia Thao is an extremely popular makeup artist and beauty influencer from Minnesota. She first started posting videos to her channel on YouTube in 2009 as a seventeen-year-old who wanted to win makeup contests. As she became a professional makeup artist in her years following high school, she continued developing relationships in the beauty and entertainment industry that enhanced her expertise and helped her channel to grow. When asked to introduce herself in an interview, she gave this explanation: "First off, before anything I'm a mother. That will always be number one. I have two boys and I'm also an army wife. I'm also a makeup artist. I feel like I'm a makeup artist before I'm a YouTuber. And I'm also an entrepreneur" (C. Yang 2018). We can see a wide range of identities that she embodies here—including gendered identities that describe her family position, as well as a distinction between her career as a makeup artist and her social media postings. Yet at the very end she also clearly affirms that she sees herself as an entrepreneur; later, she mentions that she has always wanted to own her own business, so her career is a reflection of those entrepreneurial ambitions. As a makeup artist, her thriving social media presence allows her to choose the kind of work that she wants, set her own schedule in accordance with her family's needs, and be widely recognized beyond her local community in ways that merit professional development and growth.

Aspirational Labor and Going It Alone

Another way in which the particular kind of entrepreneurship taken up by influencers is similar to other micro media industries is of course in the fact that each individual works alone, relying largely on themselves to take on every imaginable task. Sophia Thao describes the way that she produces each post:

> I do everything by myself. I film. I edit. I do the lighting. For videos, I have a whole setup, so I can flip a switch, and my background and lighting is good to go. . . . As far as Instagram posts, it's pretty much the same thing. If I have an outfit picture, I usually have my husband or a friend help me out with the right angles. When I do product pictures, I have to find a backdrop and lay out the products perfectly. I do at least 10 takes to make sure the angles are right. (Brown 2017)

This narrative is remarkably familiar in relation to other Hmong American micro media entrepreneurial ventures, ranging from newspaper to radio to television production. Each differentiated task clearly demands a specific skill set, as evidenced by the fact that within mainstream film and television industries different workers take on the roles of photography, lighting, editing, set decoration, and on-screen talent, among countless others. Influencers do it all alone, with only occasional short-term assistance, as Sophia Thao describes.

Yet this description of what goes into making a single post is only the tip of the iceberg for influencer labor, as there are countless other tasks that all need to be taken up by the individual at the helm. Fitness influencer Naomi Kong is a full-time college student, but in an interview with me she described her social media work week as equally or more time consuming than her studies: "On Instagram itself I spend about fifty hours and then on YouTube another thirty. I spent about six to seven hours every day, whether it's replying back to DMs from my followers or talking to business inquiries or interacting with followers, posting and creating captions. I consider it my full-time hustle." This description reveals the fantastically immense amount of time and effort that it can take to maintain a thriving social media presence, including not only the creation of visible posts but the behind-the-scenes tasks of interacting with followers and business contacts.

Such activities epitomize what Melissa Gregg (2011) has termed "presence bleed," where the availability of digital and mobile technologies at home have erased boundaries between personal and professional spaces. This arrangement can give workers flexibility and freedom, while also resulting in the feeling of being always on and for individuals to make other sacrifices in their interpersonal relationships and intimate lives. Micro media entrepreneurs are extremely susceptible to presence bleed, as they often work from home and are constantly juggling multiple entrepreneurial endeavors throughout the day. Another Hmong American influencer named Neng Thao described the pros and cons of working alone: "It's a blessing and a curse, it's great because you're very flexible and I can do whatever I want. It's also a lot of work. You don't have anyone to bounce ideas off of, you don't have any motivation, it's all from you. I think I like it so far, but I definitely want to build a team very soon." Many influencers have the goal of being able to hire assistants to help with certain business aspects such as public relations, or technical aspects such as photography and editing. But the reality is that when a business is centered on the personality, ideas, and voice of an individual, it can be very difficult to off-load tasks to a team.

Kong's comments also point to one of the bigger forces that shapes the way that individuals become involved in this kind of work—a concept that Duffy has called aspirational labor. Duffy's (2017b) book *(Not) Getting Paid to Do What You Love: Gender, Social Media, and Aspirational Work* centers on the way that influencers and other social media producers take on this work because it has the allure of future compensation in terms of financial and social capital. She studies the largely female workforce who are enticed by the prospect of turning their passion and flexible labor into a career in the creative industries, succumbing to the ideologies that "rationalize neoliberal workers' investments of time, capital, and labor through the promise of *eventual* capital or future success" (9–10). Duffy's in-depth investigation is ultimately pessimistic about the realities of this labor, as she reveals a wide array of disappointments and inequities within the field of digital content creation. The promise of being able to have their "dream job" is nothing but an illusion. Indeed, the majority of workers remain far from adequately compensated for the amount of labor that is taken on, and it is only a limited class of elites whose work ever becomes profitable and sustainable.

In my conversation with Naomi Kong, she affirmed that her work in social media had given her aspirations of converting her online presence into a career—she had decided to transition from her former career as a hairstylist to a new path in the world of fitness. She was working toward a personal training certificate and had goals of opening up her own gym or designing athletic wear, two potential endeavors that she could see benefiting from her strong social media presence. Yet she also conveyed a sharp understanding of the fact that she did not want to build a career around simply being an "Instagrammer," particularly since she was already picky about working with sponsors and was not interested in increasing the role of businesses in controlling her schedule or limiting her artistic freedom. Rather, she saw the opportunity to monetize her labor as being connected to the idea of growing the audience base who would one day support her fitness-related businesses.

The popular Hmong American Twitter user introduced earlier in this chapter, Phillipe Thao, also expressed skepticism about the realities of a career in social media. While social media postings had already brought him a number of professional opportunities, it was his skills as a writer and editor that he hoped to actually convert into a future career. As a recent college graduate with a degree in public relations and advertising, he had already acquired a position in public relations and wanted to keep his personal social media use separate from it. He stated to me in an interview:

> While I don't want to turn social media influencing into a job, I would like to work in either the editorial or media industry, which will allow me to create content while still being able to keep my personal Twitter the way it is. Freelance writing for *Teen Vogue* was a cool opportunity that came out of Twitter, so my long-term career goal would be either working in a similar field to that, or doing BuzzFeed-type of work. Twitter has been a great space for me to be vocal about issues important to me, has helped me network with users who work in media professions that I am interested in, and has helped me learn that I would like to work in an editorial/media job. I'm not seeking to turn my Twitter into an actual profession since I want to do more with my ideas and thoughts than just tweeting them.

In addition to his desire to increase his professional output beyond the limited affordances of Twitter, Thao also explained that he was bored by the idea of continuing to work by himself. He had no interest in ever working with sponsors or producing sponsored content because he found them "annoying" as a social media user himself. He and Kong both understood that social media work was unlikely to become an end goal in itself, and were not actively pursuing careers in the field of digital media production. Their activities online fit precisely into Duffy's (2017b) definition of aspirational labor, as they both possess a belief that "their (mostly) unpaid work, motivated by passion and the infectious rhetoric of entrepreneurialism, will eventually yield respectable income and rewarding careers" (15). But they are unlikely to fall prey to the trap that it is their identities as consumers that will help them get there. Indeed, one of Duffy's fears about laboring as an influencer is that it necessarily entails remaining "suspended in the consumption and promotion of branded commodities" (6). This is not where all Hmong American influencers find themselves. On the contrary, many have foregone the potential financial profit that could come from their postings, instead deliberately pursuing training in professional job skills outside of digital media with the goal of using their social media presence as merely a potential asset in addition to their core profession.

Branding the Self

This skepticism and distrust around building relationships with corporations is unusual within the realm of influencers. Indeed, the term "influencer" itself has always centered around the business of marketing, as it literally refers to the ability of these individuals to influence the purchasing decisions of the consumers who trust their opinion. In an era where audiences are increasingly immune to traditional forms of advertising, corporations have eagerly poured money into the promise that influential individuals can still hold sway over their followers through advertising their products on their platforms or serving as brand ambassadors. This can take many different forms, and can be facilitated through many different outlets. Some of the options for monetizing one's content include running ads on the periphery of content through programs like Google's AdSense, Facebook advertising, or WordPress advertising plugins; using click-through affiliate programs like ShopSense or rewardStyle that pay influencers every time a follower clicks on a link to purchase an item; developing sponsored content and advertorial posts where the influencer personally vouches for the product; or simply receiving free goods to be reviewed/endorsed or given away.

The ubiquity of these corporate relationships within social media has even caused the Federal Trade Commission (FTC) to get involved in order to protect consumers. The FTC's *Guides Concerning the Use of Endorsements and Testimonials in Advertising* have long advocated for truth in advertising and the disclosure of financial relationships between an endorser and a brand. In 2017, they reported that they had contacted over ninety influencers with a reminder that "influencers should clearly and conspicuously disclose their relationships to brands when promoting or endorsing products through social media" (Federal Trade Commission 2017). Because of this, the identification of influencers who engage in affiliate or branded partnerships is relatively straightforward, and Hmong American social media producers rarely evidence any of these relationships.

Yet this does not mean that Hmong American influencers do not engage in marketing. As with all influencers and social media producers, their work must be understood as largely focused on the project of transforming themselves into a brand. Indeed, this kind of labor has been recognized as a defining aspect of neoliberalism, which has converted all identities into brands and all laborers into the enterprising individuals who are solely responsible for their own success or failure. Sarah Banet-Weiser (2012) defines self-branding as a moral framework that is built on authenticity, where one's personal identity becomes part of a business strategy. This notion of "authenticity" refers to both an internal logic of being true to oneself, but also the performance of self-disclosure and maintenance of an externally legible relationship to consumer culture. As she states, "The organization of cultural meaning by economic exchange does not mean, by default, that the relationship individuals have with commodities is spurious or inauthentic; rather, that exchange is a construction of a relationship within the parameters of brand culture" (14).

In all of my conversations with Hmong American influencers, the topic of authenticity emerged as a central goal and topic of interest before I even had a chance to specifically invoke the term. This was particularly the case with Neng Thao, whose brand "Neng Now" was starting to gain significant traction through his YouTube videos and Facebook page in 2019. A recent Harvard graduate, Thao had quit his job as a science educator in 2018 to travel the world and make videos about his journey toward finding happiness. His videos focus on teaching viewers about the uncommon parts of local cultures and communities that might otherwise go unnoticed, while also reflecting on Thao's own role as a cultural interlocutor and storyteller. He originally set a goal to make videos for a while and then go back to working a nine-to-five job, but his platform started to grow in influence and he wanted to keep at it. He attributed much of his success to the value of authenticity, and had even been hired to give talks at business schools about how to develop a social media presence through greater authenticity. He described:

> The key to long-term success is just doing what you want and not caring what the audience thinks because then you're more authentic and you get people who follow you who actually want to follow you.... You hear about all the mega-successful people and people always think they should be making more money, more fame, more successful. Being authentic or making sure you're seemingly authentic is a way for people to realize they're not that different from successful people. People feel lonely when they feel less successful, so being authentic helps people feel less lonely. People develop a relationship with your brand and that helps them elevate their own brand. They realize they could be friends with you and you are a real person.

These reflections help to reveal some of the ways in which influencers understand authenticity as a quality that is not only attractive to audiences, but further helps audiences relate to and connect with the influencer.

The need to understand authenticity as more than just a buzzword can also help influencers make choices about what kinds of content to publish, and why. In the midst of a conversation about how to use social media to impress potential employers, Phillipe Thao stated: "One thing that's always worked for me in terms of growing engagement and a follower is tweeting authentically as myself. There have been times that I've tweeted things I regret, but it's always my authentic voice. I'm not just trying to impress people, it's more about connecting to people." We can see how the value of authenticity served to bolster his confidence in his own work, even if he ends up getting questioned or criticized. Such methods of self-preservation and the ability to remain unapologetic are particularly important for digital content producers, given the reality that internet audiences are known to quickly turn to criticism and abuse. Although only one of the Hmong American influencers I spoke to had experienced hate speech or threatening language, they all had developed strategies for responding to the daily realities of online flak. After all, when the product being sold was themselves, even the gentlest disagreement or demand for improvement could feel deeply personal.

This emphasis on the labor of self-branding and the authentic enterprising self have been widely acknowledged as central tenets of life within neoliberalism. Moreover, all entrepreneurs believe that they are part of the product being sold, and absolutely connect themselves to their professional success and failure. But we can also note that they mark a difference between the influencers described in this chapter and the micro media entrepreneurs from other Hmong American media industries. We have seen with Hmong American mass media outlets that the individuals working behind the scenes are often concealed from view. When the identity of the individual entrepreneur is subsumed to the professional identity of the media outlet, the project of branding and marketing become depersonalized. This form of detachment from the self from one's business enterprise can help to protect the entrepreneur from burnout and emotional exhaustion. The reality is that all kinds of media entrepreneurs are laboring to produce the illusion of a unified brand that media consumers can return to for the same consistent product. Part of their success is connected to their ability to conceal struggles and discontinuities that might actually be happening behind the scenes so that they can continue producing the kind of product that is expected.

Authentically Hmong American

With all of this emphasis on the significance of influencers creating content that is authentic, real, and true to themselves, I was intrigued by the lack of emphasis on Hmong American identity in the postings of Hmong American influencers. In my quest to analyze Hmong Americans who were popular creators on social media, I ended up examining a number of accounts that had one similarity across their content—they did not often discuss or highlight their Hmong American identities, and their audiences were largely non-Hmong. On occasion they would post an image from Hmong New Year where they are wearing traditional clothing, or would help to promote a family member or Hmong product. Yet by and large, their Hmong identities were not the center of their postings, and sometimes they never discussed being Hmong at all. This decision to underplay their specific ethnic heritage can be understood in terms of marketing and building an audience, given that the small size of potential Hmong audiences is one of the most significant factors that limits Hmong American micro media industries from expansion and growth. By refusing to include "Hmong American" as a core part of their brand, these influencers could speak to a more general audience that was potentially far larger than the reach of ethnically specific media.

This did not mean that Hmong American identity was not personally significant to the influencers, or that they would deny the significant impact their Hmong background had on their upbringing. In fact, each spoke openly to me about the importance of their Hmong culture and family in our conversations. Phillipe Thao described himself as initially finding belonging within "Gay Twitter," a flexible term for the queer community on Twitter that includes people of all backgrounds but few Asian Americans. In 2017, he started a podcast called *What's the Bubble Tea?* with a Filipinx American friend named Gilary Valenzuela. The topics of the podcast centered on Asian American culture and politics, and helped him become interested in expanding his online community to specifically include Asian Americans. As he describes: "It wasn't until the time that I started my podcast that I wanted to reclaim my Asian identity. I was really enthusiastic about diving into my sexuality and didn't really see my Hmong identity as important to myself. Starting the podcast has been a way to reclaim that identity . . . [but] I don't want to remain too insular within the Hmong community. It's nice for me to branch out." Naomi Kong also affirmed that she did not specifically target Hmong Americans or even Asian Americans because she saw fitness as something that was beneficial for everyone, and wanted to impact as many lives as possible. Yet she spoke passionately about how much she believed that her Hmong identity meant to her, and that it was becoming increasingly significant in her life.

> The older I get the more I realize it means more to me than I think. I grew up in the skin that I am, so I don't know what it's like to not be like this, but I realize how it's influenced me and the way I think and see things and just the way that I am. It is very important to me. I do believe that being Hmong American has influenced my life in more ways than I actually know and understand at this time and it reflects, it influences my way of thinking and how I live my life and how I see things. It directly influences me.

These reflections on the significance of their own heritage and background in shaping their experiences are similar to those held by all of the Hmong

American media producers I have chatted with over the course of my research. But this recognition of Hmong identity is what led others to start a form of media that could help connect the Hmong American community, producing various forms of ethnic media that are designed to speak to and for other Hmong. The tweets, videos, photographs, podcasts, and Facebook posts produced by these Hmong American influencers are designed to reach as wide an audience as possible, regardless of racial or ethnic background. In doing so, they affirm the notion that there can be an authentically Hmong American self that does not foreground ethnicity, and does not seek to be limited by Hmong American media enclaves.

These decisions can sometimes be criticized by other Hmong Americans, particularly by those who have made different decisions. When Neng Thao describes his audience, he notes that it is mostly women and includes 40 percent from outside the United States, and that he has a surprisingly large following in Panama City. Hmong Americans are nowhere within his target audience, and he is proud of his ability to speak so successfully to this diverse global community. When pressed about how his Hmong identity does get expressed through his videos, he discussed a very popular video he had made about whistling languages like the Hmong language.

People want to make sure you're unapologetically yourself, but I don't want it to seem like I'm focused on the Hmong audience in the long term. Less than half my following is Hmong, and that is one avenue to success. I'm very obsessed with the Hmong whistling language on a personal level, and people are very interested in that, but it's targeted toward the Hmong community. Then you can use the Hmong community to get it out to the broader community. Your Hmong-ness becomes a value, a way to get to second and third connections who are outside the Hmong community. You have to do it in a way that connects beyond. It's very interesting, the strategy to grow beyond the Hmong community.

This description reveals a shrewd sense of how a media producer can use connections built within their own community to ultimately expand to a more general audience, even those who may initially be unaware of cultural specificities like how a tonal language works. Yet Neng has also been questioned about how much he belongs within Hmong American communities. He told a story about attending a Hmong community event and being called out by some of the Hmong American performers who focused solely on in-language ethnic media: "I was talking to some Hmong artists and singers and they said they weren't sure I was Hmong at first because I was speaking so broadly, it wasn't just about the Hmong community. They said to me, we thought if you were Hmong, you wouldn't talk to us because you were outside the Hmong community, you wouldn't come back and talk to us." This response to the success of a Hmong

American person who does not stay focused on the Hmong audience reveals how deeply identity and media audiences are linked—these artists and performers indicate that to expand beyond the Hmong audience is akin to not being Hmong at all. Neng was dismayed by this reaction to him and his work because he felt they were wrong about who he was as a person and how he felt about the Hmong American community. But he also felt it reflected a broader sense that Hmong American artists sometimes felt like failures if they could only be successful within the Hmong community. As someone who had found success through building a broader audience outside of the Hmong community he was being criticized as perhaps not being Hmong at all, but he also saw himself as potentially serving as "proof of concept" that it was possible to do so—and that other Hmong American media producers might be able to follow in his footsteps toward developing larger followings.

This discussion of how much a person of color should discuss or reference their minority identity is a common point of stress for those who reach a certain level of fame or success, including for actors, athletes, politicians, and entrepreneurs. Many high-profile people of color are criticized for leaving their community behind, or engaging in the post-racial labor of erasing racial significance in order to be accepted. Here we see a number of Hmong American social media influencers who may occasionally reference the fact that they are Asian American and Hmong American, but choose not to make it the center of their media enterprise. Within this larger conversation about the significance of authenticity, these decisions about ethnic identification must also be understood as a sincere instantiation of their identities, histories, and representational selves. It is always the prerogative of racialized minorities to name and make visible the aspects of their personal identities that are most meaningful and relevant to them, and they are under no obligation to foreground their ethnic or racial difference in a way does not feel authentic. In doing so, they are actually helping audiences to understand the many different possibilities for what it means to be Hmong American.

The Benefits of Micro-Celebrity

As discussed thus far, the work of becoming a Hmong American influencer can be understood as grueling and largely uncompensated, and the publicity these individuals gain may open them up to some critique. While many scholarly investigations into the lives and efforts of social media influencers affirm these findings and thus remain pessimistic about the potential for exploitation, the case of Hmong Americans helps to shed some light on the potential benefits of participation as well. Within the larger context of Hmong American micro media industries, we can see that these individuals are among the few to actually find ways to expand beyond the extreme constraints and limits that all

Hmong American media entrepreneurs face. They may not be able to directly monetize their postings enough to be able to sustain themselves, but that does not mean that all possibilities for financial reward are hopeless—on the contrary, many Hmong Americans are already pleased with the fact that their social media presence has helped them to gain internships, inspire career shifts, and garner minimal financial support for their family. They have little desire to become beholden to a system of working with corporate sponsors who might threaten the relationship they have with their community of followers, so they understand that a social media presence can only be a stepping stone—not an end goal in itself. While doing so, they get to reap the benefits experienced by all micro media entrepreneurs in maintaining control over all aspects of their enterprise, enjoying the flexibility of setting their own schedule and answering only to themselves, and getting to do something that they personally value and find satisfying.

As with all forms of digital engagement, there can be innumerable personal benefits to building an online community as well. Hmong American influencers spoke with enthusiasm about how meaningful it has been to connect with people from all over the world, and many told stories about traveling somewhere new and staying with a friend they had met online. Neng Thao's project of documenting different cultures necessitates an abundance of solo travel, but he affirms that he never feels alone because he makes friends everywhere he goes and always has a friend to stay with. Not only does this counter the potential isolation that many micro media entrepreneurs can feel, but it facilitates his ability to continue traveling on a limited budget and helps him learn about the cultural offerings of each new city. Phillipe Thao also felt lucky to be part of an online community that had given him queer mentors and helped to expand his social network. Moreover, he felt that his own visibility as a queer Hmong American man could help others like him to feel less alone.

> I find that in the Hmong community we're raised and conditioned to censor ourselves and save face and preserve the family name and respect our elders. From what I've observed there are so many topics that no one wants to talk about, there's no space to talk about it as a Hmong American. So that's what I take into Twitter and my podcast, to truly speak about my own experience and my own realm. I've talked very openly about my depression and failing school and those kinds of hardships. I know everyone's experience is different, but if I can speak very candidly maybe it'll inspire a queer Hmong person who is struggling with their sexuality.

His intersectional identities bring him the opportunity to connect with people from multiple communities—queer communities, Hmong and Asian American communities, and queer Hmong and Asian American communities. His widespread visibility has more potential to actually reach someone who falls into the crosshairs of these intersecting identities, which he recognizes as a minority within a minority. But just as he has found mentorship and strength from his online communities, he hopes that his ability to share authentic truths about his experiences can help others.

Conclusion: Limited Scale with Expandable Possibilities

There is an imperative within social media influencers to always be working to expand one's list of followers, constantly striving for growth. This drive is connected to the belief that without permanent and unceasing expansion, there can never be a hope of joining the top tier of elite influencers for whom career opportunities and compensation are a reality. But as with all of the other Hmong micro media industries examined in this book, we also need to consider the possibility that achieving success at a limited scale is also a worthwhile and potentially satisfying endeavor. Not only can individuals gain the benefits described thus far, but all experiences of micro-celebrity reveal the fact that massive scale is not the only kind of celebrity that matters. We have seen how so many forms of media operate at a limited scale because the labor and time of one individual is finite, but their impact is clearly significant. The label of "micro media" entrepreneur—or, as in this chapter, "micro-influencer"—might sound like it implies a negative comparison to media operating at a larger, more influential scale. But it is the contention of this book that the label of micro does not imply a deficit, and should instead simply be recognized for all of its specific affordances, logics, and goals.

Phillipe Thao maintains a professional website that helps to establish his brand and communicate his different skills and accomplishments. Alongside his resume, the site includes a clip file of writing samples from journalistic publications, a demo from his podcast, as well as examples of graphic design campaigns and video editing. It also includes a page called "Viral" that includes six examples of times that one of his tweets, photographs, or creations made a splash—including the Hilary Duff example given at the opening of this chapter, various listicles from other websites that include his content, and an image of Thao holding a sign at an anti-Trump rally. The inclusion of these moments as part of Thao's professional accomplishments reminds us that visibility—even a limited, circumscribed moment of internet fame—mark a kind of success, particularly for Hmong Americans who are constantly suffering from invisibility. Yet the possibility of reaching a wider audience is just one of many ways that Thao can demonstrate his various skills and accomplishments within media production. The benefits that can come from media production skills, cultural fluency, technological savvy, interpersonal networks, and creativity are what mark the true potential for expansion and growth.

7

Conclusion

• •

Beyond Hmong
American Media

The world of mainstream media is increasingly dominated by large-scale corporations that hire thousands of workers and use their productivity to spread content across multiple delivery channels to millions of audience members every day. We can clearly see the impact of this shift in spaces such as the movie theater, where nearly every viewing option is connected to a massive franchise designed to churn out adaptations, sequels, spin-offs, and reboots. These properties are also frequently connected to larger projects of transmedia storytelling that link movies to comic books, video games, television series, and more, expanding the labor force, reach, and cultural power of massive media franchises. News media faces many of the same trends, as smaller news corporations have been systematically acquired by large conglomerates until only a handful of media giants are left to control an increasingly large portion of the journalism universe. And we cannot ignore the tech giants who shape media content and the way it is accessed—from streaming platforms like Netflix and Amazon to social media companies like Facebook and YouTube to the creators of hardware and software like Apple and Microsoft. The common thread across all of these forms of media and technology is that at their core, they are business ventures that must mitigate risk in order to accrue the greatest profits and financial gain. The path toward reaching this goal is consistently dependent on increasing size and scale.

Throughout this book we have seen the many kinds of media entrepreneurs who resist these trends and boldly create media outlets premised on different logics and values. Doing so has revealed the existence of shadow media ecologies that may be flying completely beneath the radar of scholars and media analysts. There are countless minority populations who have unique cultures and identities but who are generations away from creating their own blockbuster films like *Black Panther* or *Crazy Rich Asians*, or developing their own television networks like Univision or Telemundo. Indeed, when considering the problems facing mainstream media with regard to neglecting minority voices and perspectives, most solutions are still aimed at minority groups with enough resources to begin to compete in a traditional media marketplace. African Americans and Latinx communities are frequently at the center of attempts to diversify mainstream media, which makes sense given that together they comprise nearly 100 million Americans with nearly $3 trillion in spending power. While it is heartening to see the shift toward recognizing these large and powerful populations, there is much work to be done in disaggregating even our understanding of "minority communities" and asking what other voices still remain underrepresented because they are neither measured nor recognized. Niche media outlets addressing ethnic minority communities have long been part of ethnic media studies, but we cannot disregard the significant differences between the millions of tiny mom-and-pop ethnic media outlets and well-staffed ethnic enterprises like the television networks mentioned above, or other sizable outlets such as the *Chicago Defender, Latina Magazine*, or Myx TV. This investigation of Hmong American media reminds us that although there are examples of news stations, film studios, and television networks created by and for minority populations, we must still recognize the oppressively high barriers to entry that prohibit countless others.

Hmong Americans comprise a small population with no home country of their own, and this has led to a situation where their media industries are necessarily limited in size. Hmong media entrepreneurs have needed to be innovative and resourceful in order to survive. The specific media industries in Hmong American communities have helped us to identify and understand the more general category of micro media industries that span far beyond this single community. They remind us that the category of "minority media" and "ethnic media" must both be broadened to account for the many small communities who maintain media industries that do not show up on any large-scale surveys, whose audiences are not accounted for by Nielsen or Arbitron ratings, and whose media operate under a different set of norms. This concluding chapter considers how some of the findings from this book can help sharpen critiques of mainstream media while also helping us reflect on the significance of micro media and its particular characteristics and attributes. It does so by expanding beyond Hmong media to highlight and briefly introduce some of the many other examples of micro media industries that also deserve closer examination.

Multiskilling and the One-Man-Band Documentary Filmmaker

The structural limits that face Hmong American media producers are similar to those facing many other small communities, and we can see this impact on a wide variety of other media practices. One example of this is in the world of documentary filmmaking. The complexities of feature film production have traditionally required extensive crews. The average size of a movie crew on a feature film has steadily climbed over the years and it is now well over six hundred individuals (Follows 2018), including preproduction, production, postproduction, and other credited roles. Yet documentary and other forms of nonfiction media production have often been possible with significantly smaller crews, including the many indie productions that focus on niche topics and utilize only the barest skeleton crew. At this size, the category of micro media can help us to better understand what is happening in terms of filmmaking labor. For instance, we have seen the way one of the innovations required with micro media industries has been to transform individuals at the helm into multiskilled jacks-of-all-trades who can manage, produce, edit, design, and distribute multiple forms of media all at once.

This then can help us to better understand the experiences of many documentary filmmakers, such as Bing Liu. The 2018 documentary *Minding the Gap* was created through the accumulation of countless solo trips made by director Bing Liu to Rockford, Illinois, to become immersed in the local youth skateboarding community. A skateboarder himself with his own connection to the area, Liu captured the intense interpersonal dramas and awe-inspiring physical feats of his subjects by going it alone—even when he had to create his own steadycam rig that allowed him to film while precariously riding on his own skateboard. As he states in an interview, "My film was a one-man-band type of production—the lack of a crew allowed access to an intimate, trusting and emotional part of my characters' everyday lives I wouldn't have had otherwise" (Filmmaker Magazine 2018). But the results paid off with a sensitive portrait that helped his subjects open up to him about difficult personal subjects and earned the film an Academy Award nomination and a Peabody Award.

While Liu's story reveals the creative strengths of this approach, there are many other aspects of documentary filmmaking that can become a burden when one person is responsible for so many different roles. For instance, there are many cases where the "one-man-band" strategy has required that single filmmaker to be responsible for aspects like distribution and sales, in addition to creative roles such as directing, filming, and editing. In Nora Stone's (2018) examination of documentary distribution, she notes the rise of self-distribution tactics within documentary filmmaking that requires filmmakers to call attention to their own work. When we place such efforts and trends within the category of micro media as it has been established throughout this book, we can better understand the complex set of questions that this raises about issues such as sustainability and accessibility for filmmakers who focus on niche topics. For instance, if future generations of documentary filmmakers are encouraged to develop these multiple skills as a means of survival, it contributes to a filmmaking landscape where only those with privileged backgrounds and established financial safety networks can actually take on so much personal risk. As we can now see, the category of "self-distribution" has different meanings when there are multiple professionals assigned to taking on this task, rather than the filmmaker doing so on their own. It is only through considering the difference between the labor requirements for documentaries with limited crews from more traditional filmmaking practices that these struggles become apparent.

Sustainability and the Solitary Blogger

The category of micro media can also help us to better understand the blogging industry and its trajectories. The early 2000s saw the rise of many different forms of digital writing and publishing, including thousands of blogs focusing on topics such as politics, fashion, food, parenting, pop culture, news, and personal narratives. Like all forms of social media, blogs can represent the efforts of one entrepreneurial individual who takes on blogging as a side gig, or a well-staffed corporate team that uses a blog to enhance other efforts. Alongside the explosion in popularity and influence of blogs throughout the mid-2000s, many individuals jumped on the opportunity to monetize their platforms and blur the line between amateur and professional content producer. By the 2010s, however, blogs had started to fade away as users migrated to other more popular platforms and digital communities. There are many factors that are often understood as contributing to the decrease in blog popularity—including a distaste for this increasing commercialization of previously amateur platforms, and the rise of competing digital social media platforms such as Facebook, Tumblr, Instagram, and Snapchat. Yet if we consider the many individual contributors who donated so much time to the creation of these digital communities within the realm of micro media and the findings we have seen throughout the book, we can gain new insights into some of these phenomena.

One of the subject areas that saw a significant boom in the world of blogging was Asian American politics and culture. In my own research from 2014, I interviewed fifteen popular Asian American bloggers about their experiences as bloggers and specifically probed them about the emotional labor that this kind of work demanded (Lopez 2014). I found that while their political frustrations and passion were often what motivated their blogging from the beginning, the emotional toll of dealing with internet trolls and racism, the feelings of being overwhelmed and unsupported, and the realities of exhaustion and burnout all contributed to an extremely high rate of attrition and decline. Additionally, bloggers who originally had the passion to make time for this kind of side hustle would later lose the motivation to continue when they realized it would not be financially profitable, and their life priorities would naturally shift toward other endeavors. While I originally studied these factors as a way of understanding the role of emotion in relation to identity-based blogging, this kind of investigation would clearly be strengthened with an understanding of Asian American bloggers as micro media entrepreneurs. In addition to being able to consider their struggles over emotional labor in relation to other micro media industries, a number of other factors also emerge.

For instance, we have seen throughout this book that outlets helmed by micro-sized staff are distinct in the way they are simultaneously vulnerable and resilient. They are vulnerable due to the fact that so much responsibility rests in the hands of a single individual, who may face a high likelihood of becoming stressed out and exhausted by the multiple duties that must be taken on. That person can easily terminate media production, closing up shop immediately and permanently. Yet we have also seen how individual media outlets can potentially be marked by resiliency, as there is very little that can be done to threaten or persuade that individual to change course. Micro media entrepreneurs have the freedom to make their own choices with no gatekeepers barring the way, and no threat of being fired. When making decisions about their content and how it will perform, there is little need to please shareholders, investors, advertisers, employers, or employees. The motivation to continue is dependent on the individual at the helm, and the community he or she is trying to reach.

While most of the Asian American blogs that rose to prominence in the blogging heyday have dwindled to a trickle as their webmasters migrated to other roles, there is one that stands strong nearly two decades later—after starting his blog *Angry Asian Man* in 2001, Phil Yu celebrated the twentieth birthday of the blog in February 2021. While there is much to be said about the vulnerability of micro media outlets, those that survive also have much to teach us about resilience. One important aspect of Phil Yu's story is that in 2013, he transitioned from his full-time job at Yahoo! Movies to running his blog full time. To support himself, he does a yearly subscriber drive for the blog, in addition to expanding his media empire beyond the blog to include other programming such as a podcast called *They Call Us Bruce* with cohost Jeff Yang and a YouTube series called *Angry Asian America* with cohost Jenny Yang. He also frequently travels the country to give presentations at college campuses, where many students are fans of both Yu and his political messages. But through it all, he still maintains the blog—posting regular updates that alert loyal readers to current news about all things Asian American.

To some extent, Yu has been able to maintain his blog for such a long period of time because the primary format is centered on aggregating links to external content, many of which are forwarded to him by his followers. This is not to say that blogging is not a demanding task, as he accompanies each link with short write-ups and reportage, and must wrangle weekly participants to submit information as the Reader of the Week. But it contrasts with the format of more personal blogs that rely on the blogger being able to consistently mine their own personal experiences for narration, their own wardrobe for fashion tips, their own kitchen for recipes, and the like. We can see that one way that micro media entrepreneurs can maintain the longevity of their outlet is to consider the format and what kind of personal investment it might take to maintain it in the long term. When taken up in conjunction with other related projects that can help to keep the content relevant—rather than maintaining a full-time profession that is unrelated—an individual outlet can potentially be sustained for decades.

Like many of the Hmong outlets discussed throughout the book, Yu's blog has served as an important and politically meaningful contribution to Asian American politics due to the rarity of this content. Many readers learn about Asian American identities and communities for the first time through Yu's blog, and its continued longevity thus serves to diversify the media landscape even as digital consumers start to turn away from blogs. If micro media industries offer an opposing force to media conglomeration and consolidation of power, the question remains as to whether or not they encourage or facilitate the diversification of voices and perspectives or shore up existing power dynamics that are already entrenched in our media landscape. Each of the industries profiled has a different relationship to participation, revealing a wide variety of possibilities. In many ways, the creation of micro media empires can close off the potential for a diversity of voices, since it means that much of the media landscape is then owned and controlled by a limited number of voices. These individuals also skew toward the most powerful members of the community, such as men—and this is true for *Angry Asian Man* as well. But the resilience and opportunity for individuals to break in is also always available, and these diverse voices are difficult to silence.

Hybrid Media Platforms and Podfic

The goal of diversifying media production so that different kinds of audiences can see themselves and their experiences represented in the media can be one reason to persevere even in the face of financial struggles. But there are many other kinds of incentives that exist for media producers—like many forms of community media and ethnic media, micro media producers have a wide range of reasons for taking on these kinds of projects. Other motivations may include a desire to inform their community about a topic that is important to them, to form connections with like-minded community members, or to increase their own social capital. One community of media producers that frequently engages in the small-scale production of niche media for all of these reasons is fan communities. Indeed, within the realm of fan discourse and academic studies of fandoms, it is often assumed that all fannish labor is undertaken as part of a gift economy that serves to connect individuals by avoiding the cultural norms of commercialization and financial exchange. This includes the sharing of writing, videos, GIFs, artwork, games, clothing and costumes, physical objects, and commentary about beloved texts and franchises, as well as the kinds of managerial labor required to maintain fan communities. Fan fiction, or original works of fiction that are based on a specific textual world or set of characters (such as Harry Potter or Star Wars), are often held up as an example of a fan object that demands significant investment of time to create but is shared freely. Karen Hellekson (2009) argues that "gifts have value within the fannish economy in that they are designed to create and cement a social structure" (115). Because fans are often invested in the project of creating social bonds and conveying something meaningful about and for the creator, they often avoid participation in a commercial market. There are rare exceptions to this, such as the "fantrepreneurs" who sell their fan wares at conventions or through digital platforms like Etsy (Scott 2015), but it cannot be denied that there are many fan communities that operate within the sphere of non-commercial micro media.

One of the ways that we might apply our understanding of micro media industries to the world of fandom is to consider the ways in which fans are also at the forefront of developing hybrid media platforms. This stems from a number of factors that are central to fan communities—including, as mentioned, their freedom from the norms and constraints of the commercial market, the strength of community connections that can support innovation, as well as their passion for media creation in whatever form suits their specific preferences. An example of a fannish hybrid media platform is podfic, or the transformation of fan fiction into an audio medium by authors recording their reading performance. Communities of "podficcers" use fan websites like Archive of Our Own and other digital platforms to share these works, which blend the affordances of podcasts and fan fiction. While fan fiction is often celebrated as a transformative writing practice that gives amateur writers the opportunity to flex their literary skills and bend content worlds to their personal desires, studies of podcasting have been more focused on its affordances as a sonic medium that builds from the histories of radio broadcast. Olivia Riley (2020) combines these two aspects in her analysis of the way that podfic becomes a particularly intimate site for exploring queerness due to the combination of emphasis on vocal performance and the vocal bodies of the performer, as well as the common focus on sexual themes in the content of the text. A focus on queer content and the potential vulnerability of both the speaker and listener mean that the small size and scale are key factors that helped this form of media find roots and flourish—in addition to the interesting ways in which this hybrid media platform challenges our understanding of both podcasts and fan fiction.

Like Hmong American media producers, there are many other ways in which communities of fans are actively experimenting with and testing out new ways to deploy media technologies in the quest for a format that is most useful and meaningful to their specific audience. There are many kinds of fantrepreneurship, digital fan communities, and fan media products that serve to challenge traditionally accepted understandings of media platforms, and it is important to explore the meanings of these transgressions and expansions in relation to larger questions about media technologies, genres, and platforms. These new sites for inquiry and exploration demand closer attention, as we consider the way that size and scale facilitate a certain kind of adaptability and innovation.

Conclusion

In reflecting on the unique experiences, triumphs, and struggles of micro media producers, it is my hope to have inspired an increased respect for the amount of time, energy, and labor these skilled professionals put into creating media for their specific communities. While micro media industries cannot provide a solution to all of the shortcomings of the mainstream media networks that so often ignore or exclude them, they nonetheless play a vital role within our media landscape. We have seen throughout this book that micro media industries provide information, connection, and access for communities with specific needs. Yet they face unique challenges and struggles that continue to threaten their survival, particularly when so much of their labor and contributions go unrecognized.

Micro media entrepreneurs occupy a unique space within neoliberal media industries in which all professionals are increasingly required to engage in self-promotion and self-governance. Indeed, as even the largest media outlets start to rely on a growing workforce of contracted gig workers and freelancers, neoliberal ideologies locating success at the level of the enterprising individual become the norm rather than the exception. This means that understandings of micro media entrepreneurship are more important than ever. The kinds of media industries profiled in this book stand apart from the gig economy in the sense that their owners remain independent and in control of their own destiny, while also developing a robust skill set that could be of use to other professionals who are increasingly ending up in similar situations. Their unique voices and passion for injecting their perspective into spreadable media have the ability to change the lives of the communities that come to depend on them. Yet their existence also calls attention to the impact of this labor on the lives of those who are required to work alone, take on multiple jobs for survival, constantly develop new skill sets, and struggle to become part of a professional community.

One of the most important lessons I have learned from studying Hmong Americans is that there is no community that is so small that it deserves to be ignored and forgotten. As generations of Hmong move through the world, their culture and identities and relationships to technology change along with them. Media provide an important way for communities of all sizes to keep their stories, their culture, and their identities alive, and the ability of small communities to maintain sovereignty and control over the way that this happens is of utmost importance. The way that this will look and the forms that it will take may be surprising or challenging, but we must always be open to these possibilities.

Acknowledgments

I want to begin by thanking the many, many Hmong people who have shared their stories, language, knowledge, culture, food, and, of course, their media with me. At the very top of this list are my Hmong teachers from the Southeast Asian Studies Summer Institute (SEASSI) at the University of Wisconsin–Madison, Choua Lee and Seethong Yang, and my fellow students Bessy Vang, Bruce Lee, Kaia Simon, and Marcie Lee. Each of you helped me to better understand the beauty of the Hmong language and why it is important to get it right. I spent that entire summer struggling with tones and fumbling with flashcards, but at the end of it all I gained far more than Hmong language skills. Indeed, my time at SEASSI is when this book project truly came to life. Thanks in particular to Seethong for later serving as my incredibly talented interpreter; you brought so much sensitivity and thoughtfulness to our conversations with Hmong families, and I am forever grateful for your assistance.

I am deeply indebted to all of the Hmong media producers and consumers who graciously allowed me to ask questions and learn about their media and their lives. So many of you asked how this research would benefit the Hmong community, and I hope that I have lived up to my promise to write a book that college students could read in order to learn more about the Hmong people who are so often left out of the curriculum. There are also many Hmong studies scholars who have shared their expertise, research, and feedback with me over the years. Thanks to Chong Moua, Cua Xiong, Yang Sao Xiong, Kong Pheng Pha, Ma Vang, Aline Lo, Ian Baird, Mitch Ogden, Jacob Hickman, and the many other members of the Hmong Studies Consortium. I am grateful and humbled to have been a part of this research community, and excited that there are so many talented Hmong scholars who are pushing this field of study forward.

This research has been supported by a number of grants, including from the University of Wisconsin–Madison's Fall Research Competition and the semester I spent as a Race, Ethnicity, and Indigeneity Fellow at the University of Wisconsin–Madison's Institute for Research in the Humanities. These grants allowed me to have the time to conduct research and write, and also supported many research assistants who aided me in listening to and interpreting media broadcasts. This included Bouavanh Xiong, Peter Xiong, Gao Hnou Xiong, Vang Xiong, Ashley Xiong, and Mai Nou Her. I am also grateful to Ger Xiong, whose course "Exploring Hmong American Experience through Service Learning" facilitated my partnership with many of these excellent research assistants.

I have presented this work at far too many conferences, where my fellow scholars asked prescient questions that shaped the course of this work. These include conferences for the International Communication Association, the Society for Cinema and Media Studies, the American Studies Association, the Association for Asian American Studies, Hmong Around the World Conference, Hmong Across Borders Conference, Myra Washington's Race and Media Conference in Albuquerque, Derek Johnson's ice cream–filled TV conference, and others I may be forgetting. It was at conferences like these that I was able to bend the ear of amazing scholars like Aswin Punathambekar and LeiLani Nishime, who have both been tremendously helpful in strengthening the manuscript. I am particularly grateful to my advisor-for-life Radhika Parameswaran for inviting me to present this research at the Indiana University Department of Journalism and Mass Communication Colloquium, especially because it meant I could spend quality time with Choco and Kevin.

Thank you to Lisa Banning at Rutgers University Press for supporting this project and helping this book find a home, and to the manuscript reviewers who provided useful suggestions. This manuscript benefited greatly from my developmental editor Laura Portwood-Stacer, who did the embarrassingly invaluable work of helping me hone my central argument. Thanks also to Lori Morimoto for her excellent work on the index. Portions of chapter 5 appeared in articles I originally published in *Communication, Culture and Critique* in 2017 and *International Journal of Communication* in 2016.

As with all of my academic endeavors, nothing would be possible without the unceasing support of my colleagues at the University of Wisconsin–Madison. Thanks in particular to Jonathan Gray, who is not only one of my closest friends (and pandemic pod family!), but has always believed in this project and found ways to help it grow. Much gratitude also to my beloved office buddy Jeremy Morris, for letting me choose where we go for lunch and for having an open door so I can disrupt your diligent work time with gossip and giggles. Derek Johnson will always have his own chair in our living room, awaiting a visit so we can debrief about work woes and engage in a spirited round of Battlestar Galactica. I don't know how many academics choose to buy a home two blocks away from where their colleagues live just so they can spend more time together, but I do know that for me, hanging out with you all has become an essential component to achieving my ideal work-life balance. On that note, thanks to Monica, Colleen, and Leanne, who are also wonderful friends and bring much joy to my life.

There are many other colleagues who have supported me and this project over the years—Jenell Johnson, Sara McKinnon, Eric Hoyt, Catalina Toma, Kelley Conway, Jeff Smith, Timothy Yu, Leslie Bow, and Cindy I-Fen Cheng. Thanks to my advisees Jackie Land, Olivia Riley, and Lauren Wilks, who are becoming fantastic researchers whose important work and activism make me proud. Also thanks to the grad students who have invited me and Jason to join you on your volleyball teams and D&D campaigns and pundemoniums and escape room adventures—Austin Morris, Thomas Welch, Leah Steuer, Nicholas Benson (and Muscle Beach Kait), Jacob Mertens, Susan Noh, Laura Schumacher, Ceci Moffett, and Anthony Twarog. I appreciate all of our grad students for their intellect and scholarship, but it is particularly nice when we can have fun together too! A huge thanks to my instructional coach and dearest friend Theresa Pesavento, who has made far too many generous offers to help me out with everything from course design to avoiding mosquito bites to growing my first garden.

Outside of my academic support system, there are many other individuals who are deserving of recognition. I'll start with a shout-out to Matthew Fuxjager and Kyla Davidoff; during a visit to see you many years ago I first learned about the Hmong population in Madison, and without those lovely visits to the isthmus I never would have thought of applying to the job here. I also want to thank all of the members of my Feminist Book Club—Rachel Andersson, Bronwyn Beck, Bowen Close, Meredith Galemore, and Erin Haley Mocciaro. I am so grateful to the Marco Polo app for allowing me to see your beautiful faces every single day so that we can share stories and make plans for our future commune. You always asked how the book was going, even when I'm sure it got boring. I also want to thank our amazing fit fam at the Big Dane Collective and especially our coaches, who give me something (sweaty) to look forward to every day.

Finally, thanks to my family, who have listened to me talk about Hmong media endlessly. To Mom and Dad, Keith, Kelli, Gabe, Donna and Anthony, and my cherished nieces and nephews Talia, Marina, Logan, and Seth—I always wish that we lived closer so we could see each other more, but you know I am thinking about you all the time. Thanks to those of you who have tried to read my books, but I would be perfectly happy if you only read these acknowledgments and stopped here—you all have more important things to do in your lives! And of course the prized last acknowledgement, the one that always means the most, goes to Jason. You still give me butterflies in my stomach when I think about how much I love you.

Notes

Chapter 1   Introduction

1   Interviews with media producers included twenty-three men, twenty-six women, and one gender nonconforming person. They also included twenty-four first-generation immigrants born in Laos or Thailand, and twenty-four second-generation Hmong Americans born in the United States. The locations included ten interviews in central California, twenty-one in the Twin Cities, and nineteen in Wisconsin. Thirteen interviews were conducted over the phone and thirty-seven in person; forty-eight were in English and two were with in Hmong with a translator.

2   Interviews with media consumers included twenty-two men and twenty-six women. They also included thirty-three first-generation immigrants born in Laos or Thailand, and fifteen second-generation Hmong Americans born in the United States. All interviews took place in Wisconsin with Wisconsin residents; fifteen interviews were conducted over the phone and thirty-three in person; eighteen were in English and thirty were in Hmong with a translator.

Chapter 3   TV without Television

1   A brief list and incomplete list of organizations that have focused on Hmong gender issues includes: Hmong American Woman's Association, Hnub Tshiab: Hmong Women Achieving Together, Empowering Hmong Women, Hmong Women's Heritage Association, Women's Association of Hmong and Lao, Association for the Advancement of Hmong Women, Hmong Women's Leadership Institute, Hmong Women Empowerment Summit, Hmong Women Today, Viv Ncaus: A Hmong Women's Giving Circle, Freedom Inc., Hmong Women's Circle, Hmong Women's Action for Inspiration, Man Forward, and Breaking for Justice.

Chapter 4   Global Participatory Networks

1   Although the use of conference call software seems to evidence that Hmong teleconference radio programs rely on a computer and an internet connection, the

vast majority of callers use nothing but a cell phone to participate in the shows. Moreover, many of the owners of the shows (who ostensibly used a computer and internet connection to initiate the shows and sign up for a conference call number) profess to have forgotten what website they used or how it was set up, and do not seem to see their use of computing technologies as central to the functioning of Hmong teleconference radio programs. Some openly stated that they would not want the software they used to become public knowledge.

2   The Hmong language spoken across Asia includes over a dozen different dialects, but the Hmong populations from Laos who constitute the post-1975 diaspora mainly speak either White Hmong (*Hmoob dawb*) or Green Hmong (*Hmoob leeg*). White Hmong is slightly more common than Green Hmong. While there were strong differences between these communities in Laos, Hmong in the diaspora have blended cultural norms and practices are generally indistinguishable outside of language differences.

3   I was unable to speak to any callers from outside the United States, but we can assume that they are finding ways to place this international call to the United States cheaply or freely. It is possible international callers used the forms of digital telephony (Skype, Google Voice, etc.) that were rare among Hmong Americans for whom the calls are always free.

4   There are eighteen family names, or clans, in the Hmong culture. Members of the clans are often distantly related in reality, but are considered to be family in the sense that it is taboo to marry someone of the same name.

5   Such narratives should not remain unchallenged, as they are certainly vestiges of the Orientalist belief that Asian cultures are primitive in their treatment of women—a perspective that denies the patriarchal culture of the United States and problematically posits "the West" as superior to "the East." Hmong scholars have worked to dislodge these narratives by specifically examining resistance and agency in Hmong women (Vang, Nibbs, and Vang 2016). Yet here I simply echo the words of Hmong participants in this study, who state that this is how they understand Hmong culture.

Chapter 6   Alternative Aspirational Labor

1   Individuals who were interviewed include Phillipe Thao, Naomi Kong, and Neng Thao. Analysis of online interviews includes those produced for the influencers' YouTube channels, as well as many interviews conducted by Christian Yang for his YouTube series *The Grind*.

References

Abidin, Crystal. 2016. "'Aren't These Just Young, Rich Women Doing Vain Things Online?': Influencer Selfies as Subversive Frivolity." *Social Media + Society* 2(2): 1–17.

———. 2017a. "#Familygoals: Family Influencers, Calibrated Amateurism, and Justifying Young Digital Labor." *Social Media + Society* 3(2): 1–15.

———. 2017b. "Influencer Extravaganza: Commercial 'Lifestyle' Microcelebrities in Singapore." In *The Routledge Companion to Digital Ethnography*, edited by Larissa Hjorth, Heather Horst, Anne Galloway, and Genevieve Bell, 158–168. New York: Routledge.

———. 2018. *Internet Celebrity: Understanding Fame Online*. Bingley, UK: Emerald.

Achtenhagen, Leona. 2008. "Understanding Entrepreneurship in Traditional Media." *Journal of Media Business Studies* 5(1): 123–142.

Anderson, Chris. 2006. *The Long Tail: Why the Future of Business Is Selling Less of More*. New York: Hyperion.

Andrejevic, Mark. 2007. "Surveillance in the Digital Enclosure." *Communication Review* 10:295–317.

Baines, David. 2012. "Hyper-local News: A Glue to Hold Rural Communities Together?" *Local Economy* 27(2): 152–166.

Baird, Ian. 2014. "Chao Fa Movies: The Transnational Production of Hmong American History and Identity." *Hmong Studies Journal* 15(1): 1–24.

Baker, C. Edwin. 2006. *Media Concentration and Democracy: Why Ownership Matters*. Cambridge: Cambridge University Press.

Balance, Christine Bacareza. 2012. "How It Feels to Be Viral Me: Affective Labor and Asian American YouTube Performance." *Women's Studies Quarterly* 40(1–2): 138–152.

Baldillo, Aimee, Jeanette Mendy, and Vincent Eng. 2005. "Save a Hunter, Shoot a Hmong." *Modern American* 1(1): 3–7.

Banet-Weiser, Sarah. 2012. *Authentic TM: The Politics of Ambivalence in a Brand Culture*. New York: New York University Press.

Bensinger, Greg. 2012. "Talking Less, Paying More for Voice." *Wall Street Journal*, June 5. https://www.wsj.com/articles/SB10001424052702304065704577426760861602618.

Bird, Elizabeth S. 2011. "Are We All Produsers Now? Convergence and Media Audience Practices." *Cultural Studies* 25(4–5): 502–516.

Bishop, Ronald, and Ernest A. Hakanen. 2002. "In the Public Interest? The State of Local Television Programming Fifteen Years after Deregulation." *Journal of Communication Inquiry* 26(3): 261–276.

Blankenship, Justin C. 2016. "Losing Their 'Mojo'? Mobile Journalism and the Deprofessionalization of Television News Work." *Journalism Practice* 10(8): 1055–1071.

Boulden, Walter T. 2009. "Gay Hmong: A Multifaceted Clash of Cultures." *Journal of Gay and Lesbian Social Services* 21(2–3): 134–150.

Boyd, Josh. 2001. "Corporate Rhetoric Participates in Public Dialogue: A Solution to the Public/Private Conundrum." *Southern Journal of Communication* 66(4): 279–292.

Brown, Rachel. 2017. "Sophia Thao Rocks Regular Girl Glamour on Social Media." *BeautyIndependent.com*, October 13. https://www.beautyindependent.com/sophia -thao-social-media-glamour/.

Carland, James W., Frank Hoy, William Boulton, and Jo Ann C. Carland. 1984. "Differentiating Entrepreneurs from Small Business Owners: A Conceptualization." *Academy of Management Review* 9(2): 354–359.

Casillas, Dolores Inés. 2011. "Sounds of Surveillance: U.S. Spanish-Language Radio Patrols La Migra." *American Quarterly* 63(3): 807–829.

Christian, Aymar Jean. 2018. *Open TV: Innovation beyond Hollywood and the Rise of Web Television*. New York: New York University Press.

Collier, Ann Futterman, Martha Munger, and Yong Kay Moua. 2012. "Hmong Mental Health Needs Assessment: A Community-Based Partnership in a Small Mid-Western Community." *American Journal of Community Psychology* 49(1–2): 73–86.

Connery, Brian. 1997. "IMHO: Authority and Egalitarian Rhetoric in the Virtual Coffeehouse." In *Internet Culture*, edited by David Porter, 161–180. New York: Routledge.

Cormode, Graham, and Balachander Krishnamurthy. 2008. "Key Differences between Web 1.0 and Web 2.0." *First Monday* 13(6). http://journals.uic.edu/ojs /index.php/fm/article/view/2125/1972.

Couldry, Nick. 2000. *The Place of Media Power: Pilgrims and Witnesses of the Media Age*. London: Routledge.

Dabby-Chinoy, Chic. 2012. *Abusive International Marriages: Hmong Advocates Organizing in Wisconsin*. San Francisco: Asian and Pacific Islander Institute on Domestic Violence.

Depke, Jill, and Adedayo Onitilo. 2011. "Coalition Building and the Intervention Wheel to Address Breast Cancer Screening in Hmong Women." *Clinical Medicine and Research* 9(1): 1–6.

Deuze, Mark. 2006. "Ethnic Media, Community Media and Participatory Culture." *Journalism* 7(3): 262–280.

Dori-Hacohen, Gonen. 2012. "Gatekeeping Public Participation: An Ethnographic Account of the Production Process of a Radio Phone-in Programme." *Radio Journal* 10(2): 113–129.

Downing, John D. H. 2001. *Radical Media: Rebellious Communication and Social Movements*. Thousand Oaks, CA: Sage.

Doyle, Gillian. 2013. *Understanding Media Economics*. London: Sage.

Duffy, Brooke Erin. 2017a. "Gender and Self-Enterprise in the Social Media Age: A Digital Double Bind." *Information, Communication and Society* 20(6): 843–859.

———. 2017b. *(Not) Getting Paid to Do What You Love: Gender, Social Media, and Aspirational Work.* New Haven, CT: Yale University Press.

Duffy, Brooke Erin, and Emily Hund. 2015. "'Having It All' on Social Media: Entrepreneurial Femininity and Self-Branding among Fashion Bloggers." *Social Media + Society* 1(2): 1–11.

Eng, David L., and Alice Y. Hom. 1998. *Q & A: Queer in Asian America.* Philadelphia: Temple University Press.

Falk, Catherine. 2013. "YouTube and the Hmong Qeej." *Hmong Studies Journal* 14:1–64.

Federal Communications Commission. 2014. *Report on Ownership of Commercial Broadcast Stations.* Washington, DC: Federal Communications Commission. http://www.fcc.gov/document/report-ownership-commercial-broadcast -stations-0.

Federal Trade Commission. 2017. "FTC Staff Reminds Influencers and Brands to Clearly Disclose Relationship." April 19. https://www.ftc.gov/news-events/press -releases/2017/04/ftc-staff-reminds-influencers-brands-clearly-disclose.

Filmmaker Magazine. 2018. "'The Film Began as an Experimental Skate Video': Director and DP Bing Liu on Minding the Gap." *Filmmaker Magazine,* January 25. Accessed August 20, 2019. https://filmmakermagazine.com/104231-the-film-began -as-an-experimental-skate-video-director-and-dp-bing-liu-on-minding-the-gap/# .XVvov4hKg2w.

Follows, Stephen. 2018. "How Has the Average Hollywood Movie Crew Changed?" Stephen Follows (website), March 19. Accessed August 20, 2019. https://stephen follows.com/how-has-the-size-of-hollywood-movie-crews-changed/.

Freire, Ariana Moscote. 2007. "Remediating Radio: Audio Streaming, Music Recommendation and the Discourse of Radioness." *Radio Journal* 5(2–3): 97–112.

Fung, Catherine. 2015. "'Whether or Not Words Were Said . . .': Chai Soua Vang, *Gran Torino,* and the Problem of Historicizing Racialized Violence." *Social Text* 33(1): 27–48.

Gade, Peter. 2004. "Newspapers and Organizational Development: Management and Journalist Perceptions of Newsroom Cultural Change." *Journalism and Communication Monographs* 6(1): 3–55.

Gentles-Peart, Kamille. 2014. "'Fiwi TV': Ethnic Media and the West Indian Diaspora." *International Journal of Cultural Studies* 7(6): 603–617.

Gimlet Media. 2017. "Gimlet Media's 2017 Diversity Report." Gimlet Media (website), July 11. https://www.gimletmedia.com/news/gimlet-medias-2017-diversity-report.

Gitlin, Todd. 1979. "Prime Time Ideology: The Hegemonic Process in Television Entertainment." *Social Problems* 26(3): 251–266.

Gregg, Melissa. 2011. *Work's Intimacy.* Cambridge: Polity.

Hartley, John, and Stuart Cunningham. 2001. "Creative Industries: From Blue Poles." In *Humanities and Social Sciences Futures,* edited by Malcolm Gillies, Mark Carroll, and John Dash, 15–24. Canberra, Australia: Centre for Continuing Education.

Hellekson, Karen. 2009. "A Fannish Field of Value: Online Fan Gift Culture." *Cinema Journal* 48(4): 113–118.

Hesmondhalgh, David. 1999. "Indie: The Institutional Politics and Aesthetics of a Popular Music Genre." *Cultural Studies* 13(1): 34–61.

———. 2010. "Normativity and Social Justice in the Analysis of Creative Labour." *Journal for Cultural Research* 14(3): 231–249.

Hess, Kristy, and Lisa Waller. 2014. "Geo-social Journalism: Reorienting the Study of Small Commercial Newspapers in a Digital Environment." *Journalism Practice* 8(2): 121–136.

Hilmes, Michele. 1997. *Radio Voices: American Broadcasting, 1922–1952.* Minneapolis: University of Minnesota Press.

Hjorth, Larissa, and Sun Sun Lim. 2012. "Mobile Intimacy in an Age of Affective Mobile Media." *Feminist Media Studies* 12(4): 477–484.

Hogan, Mel. 2009. "Dykes on Mics: Podcasting and the Activist Archive." *TOPIA* 20:199–215.

hooks, bell. 2015. "Marginality as a Site of Resistance." In *Out There: Marginalization and Contemporary Culture*, edited by Russell Ferguson and Martha Gever, 341–344. Cambridge, MA: MIT Press.

Howley, Kevin. 2005. *Community Media: People, Places, and Communication Technologies.* Cambridge: Cambridge University Press.

Husband, Charles. 2005. "Minority Ethnic Media as Communities of Practice: Professionalism and Identity Politics in Interaction." *Journal of Ethnic and Migration Studies* 31(3): 461–479.

Jarrett, Kylie. 2014. "The Relevance of 'Women's Work': Social Reproduction and Immaterial Labor in Digital Media." *Television and New Media* 15(1): 14–29.

Jenkins, Henry, Katie Clinton, Ravi Purushotma, Alice Robison, and Margaret Weigel. 2006. *Confronting the Challenges of Participatory Culture: Media Education for the 21st Century.* Chicago: MacArthur Foundation.

Jirattikorn, Amporn. 2018. "Thai Television Dramas, a New Player in Asian Media Circulation: A Case Study of Full House Thai." In *Asian Cultural Flows: Cultural Policies, Creative Industries, and Media Consumers*, edited by Nobuko Kawashima and Hye-Kyung Lee, 167–182. Singapore: Springer.

Kafka, Peter. 2017. "VCs Don't Love Podcasting, but Gimlet Media Has Raised Another $15 Million Anyway." *Recode*, August 2. Accessed November 23, 2018. https://www.recode.net/2017/8/2/16079634/gimlet-media-podcast-funding -stripes-laurene-powell-jobs-advertising-crooked-media-the-daily.

Kagawa-Singer, Marjorie, Sora Park Tanjasiri, Annalyn Valdez, Hongjian Yu, and Mary Anne Foo. 2009. "Outcomes of a Breast Health Project for Hmong Women and Men in California." *American Journal of Public Health* 99(S2): 467–473.

Koltyk, Jo Ann. 1993. "Telling Narratives through Home Videos: Hmong Refugees and Self-Documentation of Life in the Old and New Country." *Journal of American Folklore* 106(422): 435–449.

Kompare, Derek. 2004. *Rerun Nation: How Repeats Invented American Television.* New York: Routledge.

Küng, Lucy. 2007. "Does Media Management Matter? Establishing the Scope, Rationale, and Future Research Agenda for the Discipline." *Journal of Media Business Studies* 4(1): 21–39.

Landgraf, John. 2018. Foreword to *We Now Disrupt This Broadcast: How Cable Transformed Television and the Internet Revolutionized It All*, by Amanda Lotz, ix–xii. Cambridge, MA: MIT Press.

Lee, Erika. 2015. *The Making of Asian America: A History.* New York: Simon and Schuster.

Lee, Gary Yia. 2006. "Dreaming across the Oceans: Globalization and Cultural Reinvention in the Hmong Diaspora." *Hmong Studies Journal* 7:1–33.

Leepreecha, Prasit. 2008. "The Role of Media Technology in Reproducing Hmong Ethnic Identity." In *Living in a Globalized World: Ethnic Minorities in the Greater Mekong Subregion*, edited by Don McCaskill, Prasit Leepreecha, and He Shaoying, 89–114. Chiang Mai, Thailand: Mekong Press.

Levine, Elana. 2008. "Distinguishing Television: The Changing Meanings of Television Liveness." *Media, Culture, and Society* 30(3): 393–409.

Lieu, Nhi T. 2011. *The American Dream in Vietnamese*. Minneapolis: University of Minnesota Press.

Lim, Sun Sun. 2014. "Women, 'Double Work' and Mobile Media: The More Things Change, the More They Stay the Same." In *The Routledge Companion to Mobile Media*, edited by Gerard Goggin and Larissa Hjorth, 356–364. London: Routledge.

Lin, Wan-Ying, and Hayeon Song. 2006. "Geo-ethnic Storytelling: An Examination of Ethnic Media Content in Contemporary Immigrant Communities." *Journalism* 7(3): 362–388.

Lopez, Lori Kido. 2014. "Blogging while Angry: The Sustainability of Emotional Labor in the Asian American Blogosphere." *Media, Culture and Society* 36(4): 421–436.

———. 2015. "A Media Campaign for Ourselves: Building Organizational Media Capacity through Participatory Action Research." *Journal of Media Practice* 16(3): 228–244.

———. 2016. "Mobile Phones as Participatory Radio: Developing Hmong Mass Communication in the Digital Age." *International Journal of Communication* 10:2038–2055.

———. 2017. "Asian America Gone Viral: A Genealogy of Asian American YouTubers and Memes." In *The Routledge Companion to Asian American Media*, edited by Lori Kido Lopez and Vincent Pham, 157–169. New York: Routledge.

———. 2018. "Challenges of Accessing and Preserving 'Hmong Radio.'" *New Review of Film and Television* 18(4): 489–493.

Lotz, Amanda. 2009. "Industry-Level Studies and the Contributions of Gitlin's *Inside Prime Time*." In *Production Studies: Cultural Studies of Media Industries*, edited by Vicki Mayer, Miranda Banks, and John Caldwell, 94–113. New York: Routledge.

Lowry, Brian. 2015. "'The Slap' May Help Rouse Networks to the Value of Niche." *Variety.com*, February 11. http://variety.com/2015/voices/news/nbcs-the-slap-could-move-networks-toward-quality-niche-shows-1201430339/.

Mackay, Deborah, and Kristin Smith. 2006. "Finding a Niche: Certification as a Minority-Owned or Women-Owned Contractor." *Hennepin Lawyer* 73(10): 20–23.

Markman, Kris M., and Caroline E. Sawyer. 2014. "Why Pod? Further Explorations of the Motivations for Independent Podcasting." *Journal of Radio and Audio Media* 21(1): 20–35.

Marwick, Alice E. 2015. *Status Update: Celebrity, Publicity, and Branding in the Social Media Age*. New Haven, CT: Yale University Press.

Matsaganis, Matthew D., and Vikki S. Katz. 2014. "How Ethnic Media Producers Constitute Their Communities of Practice: An Ecological Approach." *Journalism* 15(7): 926–944.

Mayer, Vicki, Miranda J. Banks, and John T. Caldwell. 2009. "Introduction: Production Studies: Roots and Routes." In *Production Studies: Cultural Studies of Media*

Industries, edited by Vicki Mayer, Miranda J. Banks, and John T. Caldwell, 1–12. New York: Routledge.

McLeod, Kembrew. 2005. "MP3s Are Killing Home Taping: The Rise of Internet Distribution and Its Challenge to the Major Music Label Monopoly." *Popular Music and Society* 28(4): 521–531.

"Meet the Team of *Hmong Today*." 2005. *Hmong Today* 2(7): 27.

Meschke, Laurie, and Kim Dettmer. 2012. "'Don't Cross a Man's Feet': Hmong Parent-Daughter Communication about Sexual Health." *Sex Education* 12(1): 109–123.

Metzgar, Emily T., David D. Kurpius, and Karen M. Rowley. 2011. "Defining Hyperlocal Media: Proposing a Framework for Discussion." *New Media and Society* 13(5): 772–787.

Molina Guzman, Isabel. 2006. "Competing Discourses of Community: Ideological Tensions between Local General-Market and Latino News Media." *Journalism* 7(3): 281–298.

Nakamura, Lisa. 2005. "'Alllooksame'? Mediating Asian American Visual Cultures of Race on the Web." In *East Main Street: Asian American Popular Culture*, edited by Shilpa Dave, LeiLani Nishime, and Tasha Oren, 262–272. New York: New York University Press.

Neff, Gina, Elizabeth Wissinger, and Sharon Zukin. 2005. "Entrepreneurial Labor among Cultural Producers: 'Cool' Jobs in 'Hot' Industries." *Social Semiotics* 15(3): 307–334.

Ngo, Bic. 2012a. "The Importance of Family for a Gay Hmong American Man: Complicating Discourses of 'Coming Out.'" *Hmong Studies Journal* 13(1): 1–27.

———. 2012b. "'There Are No GLBT Hmong People': Hmong American Young Adults Navigating Culture and Sexuality." In *Hmong and American: From Refugees to Citizens*, edited by Vincent K. Her and Mary Louise Buley-Meissner, 113–132. Minneapolis: Minnesota Historical Society Press.

Ngo, Bic, and Melissa Kwon. 2015. "A Glimpse of Family Acceptance for Queer Hmong Youth." *Journal of LGBT Youth* 12(2): 212–231.

Nibbs, Faith. 2016. "Hmong Women on the Web: Transforming Power through Social Networking." In *Claiming Place: On the Agency of Hmong Women*, edited by Chia Youyee Vang, Faith Nibbs, and Ma Vang, 169–194. Minneapolis: University of Minnesota Press.

Nichols-Pethick, Jonathan. 2009. "The Dynamics of Local Television." In *Beyond Prime Time: Television Programming in the Post-Network Era*, edited by Amanda Lotz, 156–179. New York: Routledge.

Nielsen. 2013. *Significant, Sophisticated, and Savvy: The Asian American Consumer*. New York: Nielsen.

Ogden, Mitch. 2015. "Tebchaws: A Theory of Magnetic Media and Hmong Diasporic Homeland." *Hmong Studies Journal* 16:1–25.

Papacharissi, Zizi. 2004. "Democracy Online: Civility, Politeness, and the Democratic Potential of Online Political Discussion Groups." *New Media and Society* 6(2): 259–283.

Parks, Lisa. 2015. "'Stuff You Can Kick': Toward a Theory of Media Infrastructures." In *Between Humanities and the Digital*, edited by Patrik Svensson and David Theo Goldberg, 355–373. Cambridge, MA: MIT Press.

Perrin, Andrew J. 2016. "'Since This Is the Editorial Section I Intend to Express My Opinion': Inequality and Expressivity in Letters to the Editor." *Communication Review* 19(1): 55–76.

Pew Research Center. 2011. "Asian-Americans and Technology." January 6. Accessed October 20, 2011. http://www.pewinternet.org/Presentations/2011/Jan/Organization-for-Chinese-Americans.aspx.

Pha, Kong Pheng. 2016. "Finding Queer Hmong America: Gender, Sexuality, Culture, and Happiness among Hmong LGTBQ." In *Claiming Place: On the Agency of Hmong Women*, edited by Chia Youyee Vang, Faith Nibbs, and Ma Vang, 303–326. Minneapolis: University of Minnesota Press.

Phillips, Whitney, and Ryan Milner. 2017. "The Ambivalent Internet: An Interview with Whitney Phillips and Ryan M. Milner." By Henry Jenkins. *Confessions of an ACA-Fan* (blog), March 30. Accessed January 24, 2019. http://henryjenkins.org/blog/2017/05/the-ambivalent-internet-an-interview-with-whitney-phillips-and-ryan-m-milner-part-one.html.

Plantin, Jean-Christophe, and Aswin Punathambekar. 2019. "Digital Media Infrastructures: Pipes, Platforms, and Politics." *Media, Culture and Society* 41(2): 163–174.

"Public Apology." 2015. Change.org. Accessed August 14, 2020. https://www.change.org/p/doua-chialy-hmong-tv-public-apology.

Radcliffe, Damian, and Christopher Ali. 2017. *Local News in a Digital World: Small-Market Newspapers in the Digital Age*. New York: Tow Center for Digital Journalism.

Riley, Olivia. 2020. "Podfic: Queer Structures of Sound." *Transformative Works and Cultures* 34. https://journal.transformativeworks.org/index.php/twc/article/view/1933/2553.

Schein, Louisa. 2002. "Mapping Hmong Media in Diasporic Space." In *Media Worlds: Anthropology on New Terrain*, edited by Faye D. Ginsburg, Lila Abu-Lughod, and Brian Larkin, 229–244. Berkeley: University of California Press.

———. 2004. "Homeland Beauty: Transnational Longing and Hmong American Video." *Journal of Asian Studies* 63(2): 433–463.

Schein, Louisa, and Va-Megn Thoj. 2009. "*Gran Torino*'s Boys and Men with Guns: Hmong Perspectives." *Hmong Studies Journal* 10:1–52.

Schroepfer, Tracy, Angela Waltz, Hyunjin Noh, Jacqueline Matloub, and Viluck Kue. 2010. "Seeking to Bridge Two Cultures: The Wisconsin Hmong Cancer Experience." *Journal of Cancer Education* 25(4): 609–616.

Schultz, Cindy J. Price, and Myrtle Jones. 2017. "You Can't Do That! A Case Study of Rural and Urban Media Entrepreneur Experience." *International Journal on Media Management* 19(1): 11–28.

Scott, Suzanne. 2015. "'Cosplay Is Serious Business': Gendering Material Fan Labor on Heroes of Cosplay." *Cinema Journal* 54(3): 146–154.

Senft, Theresa. 2013. "Microcelebrity and the Branded Self." In *A Companion to New Media Dynamics*, edited by John Hartley, Jean Burgess, and Axel Bruns, 346–354. Hoboken, NJ: Blackwell.

Siles, Ignacio, and Pablo J. Boczkowski. 2012. "Making Sense of the Newspaper Crisis: A Critical Assessment of Existing Research and Agenda for Future Research." *New Media and Society* 14(8): 1375–1394.

Sparks, Shannon. 2014. "Considerations of Culture and Community in the Production of Hmong Health." *Family and Consumer Sciences Research Journal* 42(3): 224–234.

Spigel, Lynn. 1992. *Make Room for TV: Television and the Family Ideal in Postwar America*. Chicago: University of Chicago Press.

Stone, Nora. 2018. "Marketing the Real: The Creation of a Multilayered Market for Documentary Cinema." Doctoral dissertation, University of Wisconsin–Madison.

Tanikella, Leela. 2009. "Voices from Home and Abroad: New York City's Indo-Caribbean Media." *International Journal of Cultural Studies* 12(2): 167–185.

Tapp, Nicholas. 2000. "The Consuming or the Consumed? Virtual Hmong in China." *Asia Pacific Journal of Anthropology* 1(2): 73–101.

Taylor, Maggie. 2018. "Celebrating 4 Years of Radiotopia." PRX Official channel on Medium.com, March 6. Accessed November 23, 2018. https://medium.com/prxofficial/celebrating-4-years-of-radiotopia-b1cd89ca04bc.

Thao, Bruce. 2016. "Dangerous Questions: Queering Gender in the Hmong Diaspora." In *Claiming Place: On the Agency of Hmong Women*, edited by Chia Youyee Vang, Faith Nibbs, and Ma Vang, 280–302. Minneapolis: University of Minnesota Press.

Thao, Steve. 1999. "Editorial." *Hmong Tribune*, November 22, 7.

Tiffe, Raechel, and Melody Hoffman. 2017. "Taking Up Sonic Space: Feminized Vocality and Podcasting as Resistance." *Feminist Media Studies* 17(1): 115–118.

Usher, Nikki. 2014. *Making News at the "New York Times."* Ann Arbor: University of Michigan Press.

Vaj, Mai. 2015. "Mai Vaj Owner." March 15. Accessed July 7, 2015. http://www.phoojywg 2009.com/mai-vaj-owner.php.

Vang, Chia Youyee. 2010. *Hmong America: Reconstructing Community in Diaspora.* Urbana: University of Illinois Press.

———. 2012. "Making Ends Meet: Hmong Socioeconomic Trends in the U.S." *Hmong Studies Journal* 13(2): 1–20.

———. 2013. "Hmong Socioeconomic Trends in the U.S." In *The State of the Hmong American Community*, 21–28. Washington, DC: Hmong National Development.

Vang, Chia Youyee, Faith Nibbs, and Ma Vang, eds. 2016. *Claiming Place: On the Agency of Hmong Women.* Minneapolis: University of Minnesota Press.

Vatikiotis, Pantelis. 2009. "Democratic Potential of Citizens' Media Practices." In *Understanding Community Media*, edited by Kevin Howley, 32–40. Thousand Oaks, CA: Sage.

Viswanath, Kasisomayajula, and Pamela Arora. 2000. "Ethnic Media in the United States: An Essay on Their Role in Integration, Assimilation, and Social Control." *Mass Communication and Society* 3(1): 39–56.

Volery, Thierry. 2007. "Ethnic Entrepreneurship: A Theoretical Framework." In *Handbook of Research on Ethnic Minority Entrepreneurship*, edited by Leo-Paul Dana, 30–41. Northampton, MA: Edward Elgar.

Wallace, Sue. 2009. "Watchdog or Witness? The Emerging Forms and Practices of Journalism." *Journalism* 10(5): 684–701.

Warschauer, Mark. 2003. "Demystifying the Digital Divide." *Scientific American* 289(2): 42–47.

Whitehurst, David B. 2015. *Tree Stand Murders.* Denver: Outskirts.

Williams, Raymond. 1974. *Television: Technology and Cultural Form.* New York: Shocken Books.

Xaykaothao, Doualy. 2015. "Hmong Commentary on 'Bad Women' Draws Backlash." *MPR News*, August 26. https://www.mprnews.org/story/2015/08/26/bad-women.

Xiong, Nzong. 2001. "A Niche and a Need: Many Hmong Seek Out Radio and Television Shows in Their Native Language." *Fresno Bee*, March 13, E1.

Xiong, Zha Blong, Arunya Tuicomepee, Laura LaBlanc, and Julie Rainey. 2006.

"Hmong Immigrants' Perceptions of Family Secrets and Recipients of Disclosure." *Families in Society* 87(2): 231–239.

Yang, Christian. 2018. "How to Become a Makeup Artist/Beauty Influencer with Sophia Thao | The Grind 004." *YouTube*, July 19. https://www.youtube.com/watch ?v=8FX_qUf73Cs&t=65s.

Yang, Eric. 2008. "Recreating Hmong History: An Examination of www.youtube.com Videos." *Amerasia Journal* 34(3): 29–35.

Zax, David. 2014. "The Young Turks and the Future of News on YouTube." *Fast Company*, May 6. https://www.fastcompany.com/3030069/the-young-turks-and -the-future-of-news-on-youtube.

Zhou, Min, and Guoxuan Cai. 2002. "Chinese Language Media in the United States: Immigration and Assimilation in American Life." *Qualitative Sociology* 25(3): 419–440.

Zhou, Min, and Myungduk Cho. 2010. "Noneconomic Effects of Ethnic Entrepreneurship: A Focused Look at the Chinese and Korean Enclave Economies in Los Angeles." *Thunderbird International Business Review* 52(2): 83–96.

Index

About the Author

LORI KIDO LOPEZ is an associate professor of media and cultural studies in the Communication Arts Department at the University of Wisconsin–Madison. She is also affiliate faculty in the Asian American Studies Program, the Chican@ and Latin@ Studies Program, and the Department of Gender and Women's Studies. She is the author of *Asian American Media Activism: Fighting for Cultural Citizenship*, editor of *Race and Media: Critical Approaches*, and coeditor of *The Routledge Companion to Asian American Media*.